THE PRIME
Leadership
Framework

PRINCIPLES AND

INDICATORS FOR

MATHEMATICS

EDUCATION **L**EADERS

D1529777

Solution Tree

LEADERSHIP IN MATHEMATICS EDUCATION
NCSM
NETWORK
COMMUNICATE
SUPPORT
MOTIVATE

Published by Solution Tree
304 West Kirkwood Avenue
Bloomington, IN 47404
(800) 733-6786 (toll free) / (812) 336-7700
FAX: (812) 336-7790
email: info@solution-tree.com
www.solution-tree.com

Cover design by Pamela Rude
Printed in the United States of America
ISBN 978-1-934009-27-7

When we move on, people do not remember us for what we do for ourselves. They remember us for what we do for them. They are the inheritors of our work. One of the great joys and grave responsibilities of leaders is making sure that those in their care live lives not only of success but also of significance.

Exemplary leaders are interested more in others' success than in their own. Their greatest achievements are the triumphs of those they serve. Knowing they have made a difference in others' lives is what motivates their own, giving leaders the strength to endure the hardships, struggles, and inevitable sacrifices required to achieve great things. Leaders who see their role as serving others leave the most lasting legacies.

Teaching is one way of serving. It's a way of passing along the lessons learned from experience. The best leaders are teachers. The best teachers are also the best learners. They know that by investing in developing others they are also developing themselves. Even so, in leadership and in life nothing that we accomplish is singular. No one ever got anything extraordinary done alone. A leader's legacy is the legacy of many, and none of those who contribute to making a difference want to be taken for granted. No one likes to be an assumption. Everyone wants to be significant.

—Kouzes & Posner, 2006, pp. 10–11

Table of Contents
■ ■ ■ ■

About the National Council of Supervisors of Mathematics and Its Members

The National Council of Supervisors of Mathematics (NCSM) is an international leadership organization for those who serve the NCSM vision of excellence and equity for student achievement in mathematics. NCSM is founded on the strength and dedication of a growing membership of mathematics education leaders. These leaders include grade-level team leaders, course-level team leaders, department chairs, district or county coaches, site-based teacher leaders, district or provincial curriculum directors, principals, superintendents, college trainers of teacher leaders, and all who work to ensure the success of every child in mathematics.

NCSM was created at the 1968 Philadelphia meeting of the National Council of Teachers of Mathematics (NCTM), when a group of urban district supervisors decided that at the next annual meeting (Minneapolis, 1969), school district leaders should gather to form the National Council of Supervisors of Mathematics to address leadership issues in mathematics. An early and critical issue for NCSM was defining the membership. The founding members chose *not* to restrict membership to supervisors, and instead welcomed all leaders and teachers of mathematics. The open membership theme has continued throughout the years; the 35 leaders who attended that first meeting in Minneapolis grew to more than 3,000 by the end of the 20th century.

As NCSM celebrates its 40th anniversary in 2008, the vision and ideals of our founders endure:

> **N: Network** and collaborate with stakeholders in education, business, and government communities to ensure the growth and development of mathematics education leaders.

> **C: Communicate** current and relevant research to mathematics leaders, and provide up-to-date information on issues, trends, programs, policies, best practices, and technology in mathematics education.

> **S: Support** and sustain improved student achievement through the development of leadership skills and relationships among current and future mathematics leaders.

> **M: Motivate** mathematics leaders to maintain a lifelong commitment to provide equity and access for all learners.

As NCSM enters its fifth decade, we continue to strive for excellence and equity for all children. Our greatest challenge is *developing the leadership knowledge and skills that will advance these central vision points.* To that end, the NCSM Board commissioned a national writing team and enlisted the feedback of numerous professionals interested in mathematics education in order to create this PRIME Leadership Framework.

NCSM's future success depends on the extent to which mathematics education leaders can fulfill the responsibilities outlined in the Framework. Can we **Network** with other stakeholders to ensure the next generation of mathematics education leaders are being prepared now? Can we **Communicate** with one another the research regarding best-practice curriculum, instruction, and assessment as we learn from one another? Can we passionately **Support** improved student achievement initiatives? Can we seek to eradicate the social injustices that prevail in our schools and **Motivate** equity and access goals for all learners? Yes, we can— and we will, because we are **NCSM**.

—The 2007–2008 NCSM Board

About the National Council of Supervisors of Mathematics and Its Members

Acknowledgments

The PRIME Leadership Framework is the result of the vision and strategic planning of the National Council of Supervisors of Mathematics (NCSM) Board at its summer 2006 leadership meeting. With the support of then-president Linda Gojak and Board members Don Balka, Ted Hull, and Ruth Miles, the NCSM Board began 2 years of intensive writing, thinking, reflecting, and research by a wide variety of educational leaders in mathematics regarding a simple question with a complex answer: As a leadership organization, what are the leadership principles, indicators, and actions that NCSM should endorse and that all mathematics education leaders should aspire toward?

During that 2-year journey, the acronym **PRIME**—**PR**inciples and **I**ndicators for **M**athematics **E**ducation Leaders—emerged. The writing team considered many other variations, but PRIME stuck. It seemed most appropriate for mathematics education leadership. To further address the complex issues inherent in a leadership framework, the NCSM Board commissioned an expanded writing team of diverse members to complete the framework in the spring and summer of 2007. The members of the PRIME Leadership Framework writing team included: Don Balka, Laurie Boswell, John Carter, Linda Fulmore, Tim Kanold, Henry Kepner, Steve Leinwand, Miriam Leiva, Tami Martin, Ruth Miles, Suzanne Mitchell, Steve Viktora, and Gwen Zimmermann. The Board is extremely grateful to each of these NCSM members for their dedication, time, energy, and effort to research and write this leadership framework. PRIME moved from an idea to reality because of their wisdom, experience, and insight.

The Board also wishes to extend sincere thanks to the many organizations and individuals in the educational community who willingly contributed and responded to drafts of PRIME in the winters of 2006 and 2007. NCSM is indebted to the many individuals who responded with deep understanding and input that significantly shaped the final document. These primary reviewers included Terri Belcher, Diane Briars, Carey Bolster, Randy Charles, Dianne DeMille, Rick DuFour, Shirley Frye, Francis "Skip" Fennell, Dan Galloway, Marty Gartzman, Florence Glanfield, Deborah Gonzalez, Donna Karstan, Jim Rubillo, Mike Schmoker, Lee Stiff, John Sutton, Dorothy Strong, and Jenny Bay Williams.

Ultimately, PRIME is a leadership framework that reflects the knowledge, wisdom, and beliefs of the NCSM Board of Directors in support of its members and their leadership journey. The 2007–2008 NCSM Board reviewed and endorsed PRIME during the summer, fall, and winter of 2007. The wisdom, insight, and feedback by the members of the Board were essential to the final development of the framework. NCSM extends special thanks to Board members

Cheryl Avalos, Jim Barta, Susan Beal, Fran Berry, Vanessa Cleaver, Ralph Connelly, Jerry Cummins, Carol Edwards, Valarie Elswick, Paul Giganti, Kay Gilliland, Donna Leak, Carol Newman, Kit Norris, and Janie Zimmer for their "above and beyond" extensive feedback throughout the development process.

We would especially like to thank Nancy Wagner and Charlene Chausis for their expertise, guidance, and support throughout the many drafts. Their work and contribution were invaluable to the project. We also wish to thank Gretchen Knapp at Solution Tree for her positive disposition, "can-do" attitude, and deep desire to make our project a reality for others.

Finally, our thanks to our families. NCSM is an organization of volunteers who have a passion for leadership—volunteers who are supported by those they love in order to do the "work" that is their passion. On behalf of the writers and reviewers of PRIME, we thank you.

—*Timothy D. Kanold, Editor for the Writing Team, President, NCSM*

Introduction to the PRIME Leadership Framework

I refuse to accept the idea that the "is-ness" of man's present nature makes him morally incapable of reaching up for the eternal "ought-ness" that forever confronts him.

— Martin Luther King, Jr., accepting the Nobel Peace Prize in 1964

Why Create a Leadership Framework?

The PRIME Leadership Framework provides a vision of what ought to be. It calls upon leaders not to settle for the current state of "is-ness" in mathematics education, but rather to lead the pursuit of a better future for every child. Student achievement in mathematics is unlikely to improve significantly beyond current local, regional, state, national, or provincial levels until mathematics education leaders assume and exercise professional responsibility and accountability for their own practice and the practice of the teachers they lead. Leadership matters. A single mathematics education leader can have an incredible impact on the development and effectiveness of others.

The National Council of Supervisors of Mathematics (NCSM) is an organization of those leaders for the purpose of leadership in mathematics education. For NCSM, leadership for equity and excellence is a call for mathematics education leaders to create school programs in which *all* students are learning mathematics at a high level. NCSM envisions a future in which no resistant patterns of differences in academic access or success exist among students grouped by race, ethnicity, culture, gender, neighborhood, income of parents, or home language. NCSM recognizes the mathematics education leader must believe it is possible to create school mathematics programs that are both equitable and excellent, and then take action to implement access to those programs.

Leaders in mathematics education at all levels of the school or district organization—people who are well trained, broadly informed, and perceptive— are crucial for ensuring attainment of high-quality school mathematics programs. High-quality programs provide access to effective teaching of important mathematics and foster high levels of achievement for every student. High-quality programs are grounded in school-level conditions that enhance adult professional development and learning, support research-informed practice, and are guided by leadership that supports the ongoing improvement of curriculum, instruction, and assessment.

As James Spillane and others have pointed out, "What seems most critical [to effective change] is how leadership practice is undertaken. Yet, the practice of school leadership has received limited attention in the research literature" (Spillane, Halverson, & Diamond, 2004, p. 3). Leadership standards documents are almost nonexistent in mathematics education, and those that do exist are vague at best. Doug Reeves (2004) notes, "In the vast majority of leadership evaluation documents I reviewed, one of two problems prevailed. Either the standards themselves were ambiguous, or performance expectations were

> A single mathematics education leader can have an incredible impact on the development and effectiveness of others.

Leadership Domains

1. Equity

2. Teaching and Learning

3. Curriculum

4. Assessment

How can *all* teachers learn what they need to know in order to ensure access, equity, and excellence for every mathematics student?

unclear" (p. 5). The NCSM PRIME Leadership Framework identifies specific principles, indicators, knowledge, and skills necessary to lead other adults beyond the current status of student performance in mathematics into a focused, more equitable and successful future. This framework for the professional practice of mathematics education leadership actions can be used to meet the needs of novice leaders as well as to enhance the skills of veteran leaders. It serves as a tool to guide conversations and actions about leadership around indicators of exemplary practice, and it provides the language, focus, and actions for professional conversations with colleagues in the context of the workplace.

The PRIME Leadership Framework aims to describe actions for mathematics education leaders across all settings, preK–12, in all of its complexity. It begins by identifying the key leadership *principle* in each of four domains of mathematics leadership: equity, teaching and learning, curriculum, and assessment. It goes on to identify three specific *indicators* of leadership in each domain. Each indicator is further broken down into specific actions that fall on a continuum of *three stages of leadership growth* ranging from knowing and modeling leadership, to collaborating and implementing structures for shared leadership on a local level, to advocating and systematizing improvements into the wider educational community. The framework concludes with tools for reflection, self-evaluation, and discussion.

Underlying Assumptions of the Framework

The PRIME Leadership Framework does not describe or endorse any specific leadership style. Just as there is an art and a science to teaching well, there is also an art and a science to leading well. The framework is intended to engage leaders in conversations about *what* should be the focus of individual and collective leadership actions, energy, and effort, and seeks to expand the role of teacher leaders in mathematics education. PRIME is a "what to do" document and not a prescriptive "how to do" or "how to be" document. Accordingly, the PRIME Framework views leadership responsibility as founded upon three essential themes:

1. Success for every student, teacher, and leader

2. Research-informed teacher actions

3. Teacher collaboration and professional learning

Success for Every Student, Teacher, and Leader

The National Council of Teachers of Mathematics' *Principles and Standards for School Mathematics* (2000) asks two penetrating questions: How can *all* students have access to a high-quality mathematics education? And, how can *all* teachers learn what they need to know in order to ensure access, equity, and excellence for every mathematics student? NCSM believes mathematics education leaders must bring a laser-like focus to closing student achievement gaps in expected learning outcomes; closing student access and opportunity gaps to learn; building teacher responsibility for student learning; presenting a coherent curriculum; and creating consistent rigor, alignment, and analysis of student assessments. The comprehensive nature of leadership has important implications for the pursuit of best-practice experiences for every student and every teacher. When these conditions exist, the result is significant student learning across a wide range of school settings.

Research-Informed Teacher Actions

As mathematics education leaders pursue significant improvement in student achievement, they understand it is more likely to occur when mathematics teachers take actions toward research-informed best practices. Therefore, the mathematics education leader must lead the way and teach to the understanding and knowledge of these practices. The PRIME Leadership Framework is grounded in a body of research and literature that identifies effective teaching practices and actions and indicates references as appropriate. NCSM recognizes there are limits to available research evidence, however; accordingly, the framework is also built upon recommendations from experts in the leadership of equity, teaching and learning, curriculum, and assessment around actions that lead to success for every child. Ultimately, leaders must ensure that teacher actions translate from "all students can learn" to "each student will achieve."

> Ultimately, leaders must ensure that teacher actions translate from "all students can learn" to "each student will achieve."

Teacher Collaboration and Professional Learning

The Glenn Commission Report for the National Commission on Mathematics and Science Teaching for the 21st Century (2000) indicated that the most direct route to improving mathematics and science achievement for *all* students is improved mathematics and science *teaching*. In addition, findings from the National Commission on Teaching and America's Future (2003) indicated that quality teaching *requires* collegial interchange within the norm of professional learning communities. Thus, communities of adult learning are the building blocks that will establish a new foundation in America's schools.

> Communities of adult learning are the building blocks that will establish a new foundation in America's schools.

These two reports provide a clear vision of the future *necessity* for mathematics education leaders to create, support, and ensure the collaborative structures and culture necessary for leading adult learning. Furthermore, this adult learning must be shared and guided by research-informed best practices in mathematics curriculum, instruction, and assessment as teachers move toward "deprivatizing their practice [and] work together to continuously improve their instruction" (Fullan, 2007, p. 35). The leadership of well-designed and implemented professional learning communities of teachers and leaders will be "a powerful means of seamlessly blending teaching and professional learning in ways that produce complex, intelligent behavior in all teachers" (Sparks, 2005, p. 156).

The Framework

Quality teaching in all classrooms necessitates skillful leadership at the community, district, school, and classroom levels . . . These leaders make certain that their colleagues have the necessary knowledge and skills and other forms of support that ensure success . . . These leaders read widely, participate in learning communities, attend workshops and conferences, and model career-long learning by making their learning visible to others.

—National Staff Development Council, 2001, p. 8

The Leadership Principles

The NCSM PRIME Leadership Framework is based upon four essential principles of leadership that drive an improved future for mathematics education.

Equity Leadership

Principle 1: Ensure high expectations and access to meaningful mathematics learning for every student.

Teaching and Learning Leadership

Principle 2: Ensure high expectations and access to meaningful mathematics instruction every day.

Curriculum Leadership

Principle 3: Ensure relevant and meaningful mathematics in every lesson.

Assessment Leadership

Principle 4: Ensure timely, accurate monitoring of student learning and adjustment of teacher instruction for improved student learning.

These four principles emerge from the National Council of Teachers of Mathematics' (2000) *Principles and Standards for School Mathematics* and provide a coherent focus for our leadership energy, accountability, and effort. No matter what term is used—*principles, vision, mission, legacy, dreams, goals,* or *personal agenda*—the intent of these four leadership principles is the same: Mathematics education leaders must be able to ensure a better future for every student through initiating adult actions focused on improved student achievement.

Action Indicators of Leadership

NCSM recognizes that the leadership of a vision for a better future requires *action.* Thus, 3 research-informed indicators of leadership accompany each principle, for a total of 12 indicators. These indicators describe the conditions that must exist and the leadership actions that must be taken to move toward a deep, sustained implementation of the principle. Ultimately, leadership actions that seek to erase inequities in student mathematics learning experiences will lead to the implementation of the 12 indicators for improved student achievement.

The leadership of a vision for a better future requires *action*.

The PRIME Leadership Framework

Principle	Indicator 1	Indicator 2	Indicator 3
Equity Leadership	Every teacher addresses gaps in mathematics achievement expectations for all student populations.	Every teacher provides each student access to relevant and meaningful mathematics experiences.	Every teacher works interdependently in a collaborative learning community to erase inequities in student learning.
Teaching and Learning Leadership	Every teacher pursues the successful learning of mathematics for every student.	Every teacher implements research-informed best practices and uses effective instructional planning and teaching strategies.	Every teacher participates in continuous and meaningful mathematics professional development and learning in order to improve his or her practice.
Curriculum Leadership	Every teacher implements the local curriculum and uses instructional resources that are coherent and reflect state standards and national curriculum recommendations.	Every teacher implements a curriculum that is focused on relevant and meaningful mathematics.	Every teacher implements the intended curriculum with needed intervention and makes certain it is attained by every student.
Assessment Leadership	Every teacher uses student assessments that are congruent and aligned by grade level or course content.	Every teacher uses formative assessment processes to inform teacher practice and student learning.	Every teacher uses summative assessment data to evaluate mathematics grade-level, course, and program effectiveness.

Stages of Leadership Development

Leadership is about learning that leads to constructive change. Learning is among participants and therefore occurs collectively. Learning has direction toward a shared purpose. Leading is a shared endeavor . . . the learning and leading journey must be shared; otherwise shared purpose and action are never achieved.

—Lambert, 1998, p. 9

The individual mathematics education leader cannot do it alone. Collaboration is a critical master skill that enables teacher teams at the department, school, or district level to function effectively. A hallmark of teacher leadership is the ability to help teachers collaborate with one another: "Teacher leaders must enlist colleagues to support their vision, build consensus among diverse groups of educators, and convince others of . . . the feasibility of this general plan for improvement" (Danielson, 2007, p. 16). Mathematics education leaders must foster collaboration by engaging teachers in collaborative activities and promoting a culture that builds trust and consensus. Therefore, each of the indicators is described in three "stages" of actions on a leadership continuum.

Know and Model

Stage 1: Leadership of Self—Leadership of self-knowledge, awareness, development, and modeling of the 12 leadership indicators; the leader is respected for his or her own teaching and learning skills. This is the "know and model" stage of leadership growth and development.

Collaborate and Implement

Stage 2: Leadership of Others—Leadership of all students and teachers within the mathematics program; leadership and development of other teachers, teams of teachers, and administrators toward full knowledge and development of each of the 12 leadership indicators; the leader is respected for his or her interpersonal skills and commitment for leading change among teams of teachers and colleagues. This is the "collaborate and implement" stage of leadership development.

Advocate and Systematize

Stage 3: Leadership in the Extended Community—Leadership of district, state, province, or beyond reform efforts through sustained deepened systemic implementation of each of the 12 leadership indicators. The leader is respected for his or her influence and engagement with an expanded community of educational stakeholders. This is the "advocate and systematize" stage of leadership and development.

Although Stage 1 is a self-awareness stage of leadership, a passion for acting upon, modeling, and teaching new knowledge builds the credibility and trust necessary to cross into Stage 2 leadership of others. It should be the aim of every mathematics education leader, regardless of the scope of job position and responsibility, to pursue and experience the impact of Stage 2 leadership. Subsequently, if appropriate to job or career expectations or responsibilities, the leadership actions in Stage 2 could lead to the opportunity for effective teaching and leading beyond the leader's normal arena of influence, that is, Stage 3. Finally, experiences in Stage 3 could lead to discussions and expanded awareness that subsequently generate new knowledge for Stage 1 and Stage 2 development, thus beginning the cycle of leadership growth and learning anew (see Figure 1). It is quite possible for mathematics education leaders to be acting at Stage 3 for certain indicators while still processing new information in Stage 1 for other indicators.

No doubt, leadership is complex. The ambitious vision of leadership in the PRIME Framework may take a lifetime of self-learning combined with an ongoing passion and push for systems change in a continuous effort to teach others how to lead. The hazards of leading effective mathematics education change for improved student achievement will probably never disappear. It is a continuous process of growth and learning, as Figure 1 illustrates. The National Council of Supervisors of Mathematics has created the PRIME Leadership Framework both to validate the current work of all mathematics education leaders and to focus future actions and leadership growth on the goals of social justice: providing meaningful and successful mathematics learning for every student.

> It should be the aim of every mathematics education leader, regardless of the scope of job position and responsibility, to pursue and experience the impact of Stage 2 leadership.

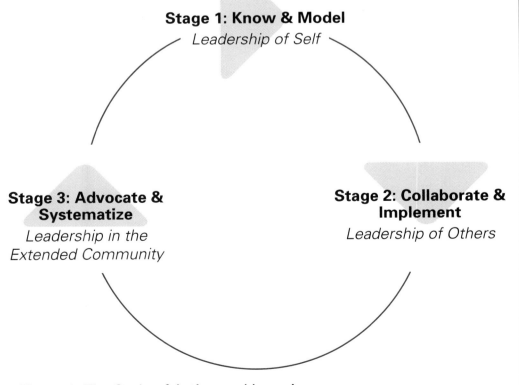

Stage 1: Know & Model
Leadership of Self

Stage 3: Advocate & Systematize
Leadership in the Extended Community

Stage 2: Collaborate & Implement
Leadership of Others

Figure 1: The Cycle of Action and Learning

Equity Leadership

Principle 1:
Ensure high expectations and access to meaningful mathematics learning for every student.

Indicator 1:

Every teacher addresses gaps in mathematics achievement expectations for all student populations.

Indicator 2:

Every teacher provides each student access to relevant and meaningful mathematics experiences.

Indicator 3:

Every teacher works interdependently in a collaborative learning community to erase inequities in student learning.

The NCSM Vision of Equity Leadership

A growing body of research makes it clear poverty and ethnicity are not the primary causal variables related to student achievement… leadership, teaching and adult actions matter. Adult variables, including the professional practices of teachers and the decisions leaders make can be more important than demographic variables.

—Reeves, 2006, p. xxiii

A vision for equity begins with understanding our leadership responsibility to seek out and erase biases and inequities that exist in student learning and assessment experiences. Time and again, too many students—especially those who are English language learners, are poor, disabled, members of minorities, or female—are victims of low expectations by mathematics teachers and by programs with barriers of access to the best school curriculum. Students who do not have access to a *rigorous* and *coherent* curriculum that holds high expectations for each student will have limited opportunities available to them later in school and in life. Leaders in mathematics education have an obligation to provide students with a mathematics curriculum and learning experience that prepare them for their future, whatever that may be. As Kati Haycock (2001) indicates, "to increase the achievement levels of minority and low-income students, we need [leaders] to focus on what really matters: high standards, a challenging curriculum, and good teachers."

It is the responsibility of mathematics education leaders to ensure underperforming student populations are identified and to provide teachers with the resources, structures, and accountability to address the identified gaps in student achievement and identified gaps in access to the curriculum. More specifically, it is imperative leaders help all teachers to collaboratively monitor the progress of traditionally underrepresented populations and create strategic plans to raise the achievement of all students, especially those who are underperforming. Mathematics education leaders are responsible for leading teachers out of private practice into a collaborative working culture focused on making thoughtful and consistent decisions about curriculum, instruction, and assessment that will meet the unique needs of all students while at the same time helping students develop deep and connected mathematical understandings.

Leaders need to eliminate practices that begin tracking students in the primary grades or lock students into particular levels of mathematical study, thereby essentially precluding opportunities to learn the mathematics necessary to open future opportunities for success. Effective leaders diminish barriers that limit student access to rigorous mathematics and at the same time ensure that every student is taught by highly qualified and well-informed mathematics teachers.

Leaders in mathematics education have an obligation to provide students with a mathematics curriculum and learning experience that prepare them for their future, whatever that may be.

Action Indicators for Equity Leadership

The indicators for NCSM's leadership standard for equity focus on the following key issues:

- Ensuring high expectations for each student

- Providing strong intervention and support for each student

- Orchestrating continuous improvement of achievement for each student

For every student to succeed, mathematics teachers must work together by grade or course level to build a foundation of challenging mathematics that present students with rich, engaging mathematical tasks and require higher-order thinking. Mathematical experiences must be meaningful and relevant; that is, the mathematics we teach should connect to student knowledge and personal experiences. Thus, leaders need to define effective teaching beyond content knowledge and classroom environment to one of developing and nurturing student, family, and community relationships by infusing culturally relevant, engaging, rigorous, yet accessible mathematics tasks into instruction (Haberman, 1997; Strutchens, 2000). It is up to the mathematics education leader to help classroom teachers create learning environments that place a high value and focus on student discourse. In these environments, teachers ask all students high-level, probing questions, while also providing differentiated instruction to support every child's learning.

PRIME leaders also understand that if *every* student is to achieve high levels of mathematical skills and understanding, teachers must collectively and critically examine meaningful data—data that will identify where students are underperforming and provide direction for action and intervention. When used wisely, data on achievement, participation, and access to the curriculum help to address inequity in a straightforward and constructive way (Chu Clewell, 1999). Using research-informed best practices, the leader determines how best to address the needs of students and works with individual teachers as well as teacher teams to make instructional and curricular changes that will hold all students to high standards and expectations.

Equity Indicator 1

■ ■ ■ ■

Every teacher addresses gaps in mathematics achievement expectations for all student populations.

Leadership of Self

Leadership of Others

Leadership in the Extended Community

Stage 1 leaders will:

- Identify and analyze student achievement data for various populations.

- Develop and apply knowledge about how to meet the diverse needs of all student populations.

- Provide specific attention to those students farthest from expected standards of rigor and achievement.

Stage 2 leaders will:

- Engage teacher teams to collaboratively establish targeted benchmarks for improved student performance in each area of the mathematics program.

- Engage grade-level and course-based teacher teams in a process of analyzing student achievement data in order to monitor student achievement across all populations.

Stage 3 leaders will:

- Ensure the implementation of a systemic plan for the continuous improvement of student achievement across all populations throughout the district, region, or province.

- Monitor the level of attainment of targeted benchmarks, use analysis of results to inform and improve practice, and publicly celebrate successful results with the extended school community.

Stage 1: Know and Model

The Stage 1 leader's first step is to determine areas where specific student achievement gaps exist within the school mathematics programs. Traditionally underrepresented groups have included, but are not limited to, Latinos, African Americans, Native Americans, females, and students who have low socioeconomic status. This task is accomplished by collecting and disaggregating data from standardized tests and local assessments. Analysis of the data helps to identify which subpopulations are lagging in achievement and where resources might be focused. Additionally, a critical scrutiny of the data by the leader generates critical "opportunity to learn" questions, such as "What percent of our students are in 'gifted' mathematics programs, and does the student demographic make-up in these programs reflect the overall school population?" and "How can we increase student opportunity to access college preparatory mathematics classes in middle school and high school?"

As more questions are asked and more data analyzed, the Stage 1 leader researches and learns about resources, methodologies, and programs that will best meet the needs of underperforming students, including students served by English language learner and special education programs. The Stage 1 leader purposefully reflects upon, develops, and models an understanding of social justice issues contributing to educational inequities, such as racism, social class, and gender bias, and recognizes his or her own biases as well.

Stage 2: Collaborate and Implement

At Stage 2, the leader works with individual teachers as well as teams of teachers to evaluate the effectiveness of instruction and curricular programs. The leader helps teachers to do the following:

- Learn how to use data as a tool to make instructional decisions.

- Learn how to design effective assessments that capture meaningful information about student learning.

- Develop and implement research-informed instructional strategies to differentiate the learning needs for each subpopulation of students.

- Develop formative and summative assessments as tools to determine the effectiveness of the curriculum.

Using the assessment data, teachers collaborate to set benchmarks for student performance and then use the benchmarks to measure progress and make changes to instruction and curriculum as needed. The Stage 2 leader works with teachers to develop articulated and measurable student achievement goals. As teachers make informed decisions and tie those goals to areas of inequity in the school, the leader celebrates successful movement toward those goals with the teachers.

The Stage 2 leader works with teachers to develop articulated and measurable student achievement goals.

Stage 3: Advocate and Systematize

At Stage 3, the leader continues to use data to monitor students' progress and makes data collection and analysis of student performance an integral part of teacher discussions and goal-setting. In addition, teachers are required to collaborate and work toward creating equitable experiences for students that challenge each student to develop a conceptual understanding of mathematics. What differentiates Stage 3 is the leader's attention to and sharing of systems and processes. He or she works to establish a coherent plan aimed to eliminate gaps from expected learning and to hold adults involved accountable for the increasing achievement of every student throughout the district, region, or province.

Stage 3 leaders create dialogue around issues of bias and cultural differences that impact student learning and broker teacher actions that will address gaps in student learning experiences. Leaders at this stage share results from high-performing mathematics programs with other collaborative teacher teams and exchange this knowledge with other schools, parents, and communities.

The Stage 3 leader publicly shares longitudinal trend data for the school or district in order to measure and monitor student achievement gains in academic performance.

Equity Indicator 2

∎ ∎ ∎ ∎

Every teacher provides each student access to relevant and meaningful mathematics experiences.

Stage 1 leaders will:

- Develop, model, and apply knowledge and strategies that reflect the importance of connecting mathematics to the context of students' experiences.

- Identify patterns of student access to the mathematics curriculum.

Stage 2 leaders will:

- Engage teachers in the development and implementation of lessons that reflect the importance of relevant, meaningful mathematics.

- Engage teachers to create and implement strategies that improve student access to the mathematics curriculum, and ensure teachers act on those strategies.

Stage 3 leaders will:

- Ensure the school, district, regional, or provincial mathematics program is vertically and horizontally aligned and reflects relevant and meaningful content.

- Ensure implementation of school, district, regional, or provincial policy and practice that limit tracking while providing access, opportunity, and proactive intervention for students across all populations.

Leadership of Self

Leadership of Others

Leadership in the Extended Community

Students should be assigned work worthy of their best effort—work that connects to their experiences.

Stage 2 leaders help teacher teams reframe inequity as not an "achievement gap," but rather an "opportunity gap" (Flores, 2007).

Stage 1: Know and Model

The Stage 1 leader understands the tenets of the National Council of Teachers of Mathematics' (2000) *Principles and Standards for School Mathematics*. The leader recognizes that learning mathematics goes beyond learning mathematical facts and skills to acquiring and applying content knowledge. Accordingly, students should be assigned work worthy of their best effort—work that connects to their experiences. Most importantly, mathematics homework and "work" in general need to be authentic and engaging to a child's world and culture (Darling-Hammond, 2006). Rich mathematical understandings result when students learn mathematics that builds from previous knowledge and connects to their own experiences. The mathematics leader understands and models mathematics lessons that engage students and include lesson elements considered important and meaningful to the context and culture of the student.

A Stage 1 leader also understands that tracking as a policy and practice creates inequities. Students in "higher" tracks often receive access to higher level mathematics focused on developing understanding, while "lower" track classes often focus on computational skills and low-level mastery (Oakes, 1985). Thus, tracking severely limits students' access to learn meaningful mathematics, especially among minority students (Strutchens et al., 2004; Wilkins et al., 2006). It is the responsibility of the leader to provide opportunities for students to access the school's best curriculum.

Stage 2: Collaborate and Implement

Stage 2 leaders work with teachers and teacher teams to create and implement lessons that value what students already know. They help teachers create engaging activities that require students to communicate and problem-solve (Romberg & Kaput, 1999). The leader expects instruction will reflect the varied learning styles of students while simultaneously engaging them in rich, meaningful, and culturally relevant mathematics.

Leaders at Stage 2 help teachers to create a culture in which every student partakes in meaningful mathematical activities involving problem-solving, communication, reasoning, and collaboration. The leader ensures that every teacher creates a learning environment that challenges and inspires students to commit their best effort toward learning mathematics each day. The leader encourages the building of a classroom climate and personal relationships that lead to the sense of community, ownership, and risk-taking necessary to engage students (Saphier, 2005) in rich discourse about relevant mathematical content. Stage 2 leaders ensure teachers do not allow any student to disengage from the learning experience. Inequities are caused when high-level, thought-provoking questions are not asked of each and every student and when student discourse and collaboration in the classroom are not the norm.

Stage 2 leaders help teacher teams reframe inequity as not an "achievement gap," but rather an "opportunity gap" (Flores, 2007). The achievement gap views groups of students through a deficit lens. By leading teacher-team dialogue and analysis of *opportunity and access* for all students, Stage 2 leaders focus their energy on making the vision of equity a reality and begin to eliminate the access barrier and subsequent damage caused by tracking.

Stage 3: Advocate and Systematize

The Stage 3 leader examines the overall district mathematics program to ensure a coherent curriculum that is vertically and horizontally aligned. The leader advocates policies that ensure access to high-level mathematics for every student across all schools in the district or province. Policies and practices that track students or prevent access to higher-level mathematics are eliminated or severely limited. Additionally, programs are created for early identification of students who are not succeeding to ensure support and research-informed interventions for these students.

Because teacher quality has a large impact on student understanding of mathematics, the Stage 3 leader ensures mathematics instruction is provided by teachers who possess the mathematical knowledge about the content and curriculum necessary to meet the needs of every student. The Stage 3 leader provides access to teacher staff development that will hold every teacher accountable for learning the skills necessary to maximize student learning. The Stage 3 leader creates programs, policies, and practices that inform guidance counselors, administrators, and parents of the post-secondary and career importance of meaningful, relevant, and rigorous mathematics. Finally, a leader at this stage engages teachers and teacher leaders at a district, regional, state, national, or provincial level in discourse regarding methods for obtaining greater access, opportunity, and successful interventions for students across all populations.

Equity Indicator 3

■ ■ ■ ■

Every teacher works interdependently in a collaborative learning community to erase inequities in student learning.

Leadership of Self

Leadership of Others

Leadership in the Extended Community

Stage 1 leaders will:

- Recognize, understand, and model the components of a professional learning community.

- Develop a results-driven culture, and participate in a collaborative teacher team for mathematics program improvement.

Stage 2 leaders will:

- Collaborate with teachers to create the support and structures necessary to implement a professional learning community.

- Support the learning of teachers to work as a professional learning community in order to monitor gains in student achievement for every student population.

Stage 3 leaders will:

- Advocate for and ensure a systemic implementation of a professional learning community throughout all aspects of the mathematics curriculum, instruction, and assessment at the school, district, regional, or provincial level.

Stage 1: Know and Model

A Stage 1 leader becomes informed of the components of a professional learning community and how such a culture focuses on improved student learning through the collaborative and interdependent work of teachers who use data to guide curricular and instructional decisions. The Stage 1 leader is aware of the importance of creating a shared vision and culture in which teachers seek to continuously improve instruction and grow professionally together. The leader models participation on a team. As part of this culture, the leader realizes that teachers working alone in their classrooms develop inconsistencies in instructional practices and rigor and create inequity in student learning experiences (Weissglass as cited in Ferrini-Mundy et al., 1998). Specifically, it is essential that teachers work collaboratively, focusing on student learning and engagement with meaningful mathematics content. The Stage 1 leader recognizes that improved student performance is greatly impacted by teams of teachers working together toward common goals and measuring progress as they share and discuss issues of practice (Marzano, Waters, & McNulty, 2005), and acts as a model for these discussions with other teachers.

As part of this culture, the leader realizes that teachers working alone in their classrooms develop inconsistencies in instructional practices and rigor and create inequity in student learning experiences (Weissglass as cited in Ferrini-Mundy et al., 1998).

Stage 2: Collaborate and Implement

A Stage 2 leader uses the acquired knowledge about professional learning communities to create teams of teachers that focus their collaborative work on student achievement and gains in mathematical performance. The leader understands the definition of a professional learning community team: *educators working interdependently to achieve common goals for which they are mutually accountable.*

Equity in student learning requires schools to be "restructured to become genuine learning organizations for both students and teachers" (Darling-Hammond, 1996, p. 198). As part of their ongoing professional learning, teachers should collaborate to:

- Design and create lessons and formative assessments as a means to examine student performance and improve teacher practice.

- Examine and modify teaching practices and strategies that will inspire students and increase understanding.

- Develop and expand their knowledge base regarding the impact of culturally responsive instruction on student learning and achievement.

- Focus on underserved populations, integrate research-informed best-practice instructional strategies, collaboratively monitor the mathematics achievement of every student, and intervene for students who require additional time and support to succeed.

The Stage 2 leader will establish the conditions necessary to ensure teachers try new strategies and use data to measure their success. Stage 2 leaders of professional learning communities "balance the desire for professional autonomy with the fundamental principles and values that drive collaboration, mutual [assessment], and accountability" (Reeves, 2005, p. 48).

The leader systematically attacks the barrier of mindless precedent.

Stage 3: Advocate and Systematize

A Stage 3 leader identifies organizational and district barriers that prevent adult action toward erasing inequity in the teaching and learning of mathematics. The mathematics educational leader sends a consistent and clear message: "The purpose of this school or district is to ensure that every student learns at high levels—to ask, what is best for each student? All stakeholders must work together to identify the needs and context of learning for our most mathematically disadvantaged students, support them for success, and hold them responsible and accountable to the same high standards of the entire student population."

The leader systematically attacks the barrier of mindless precedent exhibited by the prevailing cultural ethos of "but that's the way we've done it in the past" or "if it ain't broke, don't fix it" or "just leave me alone and let me teach." Using national, state, province, or district data, the Stage 3 leader focuses change and energy into actions that will impact student learning beyond the status quo. Minimally, these actions would include:

- Common instructional goals for each course

- Frequent monitoring of each and every student's learning

- Support and intervention for students experiencing difficulty learning

- Open parental communication about student progress

- Support for collaborative teacher teams analyzing student achievement to inform instructional adult practices (DuFour, Eaker, & DuFour, 2005)

The Stage 3 leader communicates expertly regarding all issues of equity and develops professional learning communities of highly engaged teachers to examine critically the social, political, and cultural causes of the access, opportunity, and achievement gaps that exist. Stage 3 leaders seek to eradicate biases and inequities in student learning experiences and share knowledge of successful strategies to do so with others in the educational community.

Teaching and Learning Leadership

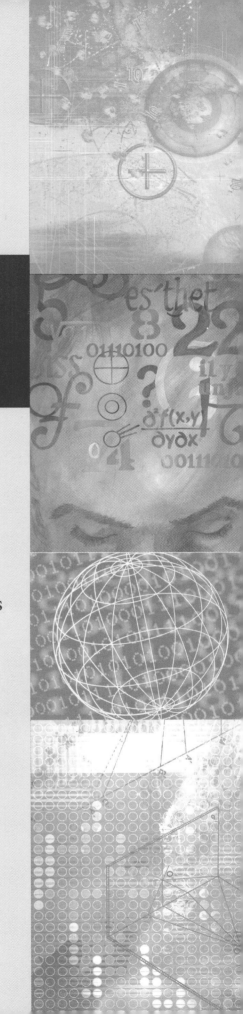

Principle 2:

Ensure high expectations and access to meaningful mathematics instruction every day.

Indicator 1:

Every teacher pursues the successful learning of mathematics for every student.

Indicator 2:

Every teacher implements research-informed best practices and uses effective instructional planning and teaching strategies.

Indicator 3:

Every teacher participates in continuous and meaningful mathematics professional development and learning in order to improve his or her practice.

The NCSM Vision of Teaching and Learning Leadership

The one factor that surfaced as the single most influential component of an effective school is the individual teachers within the school.

—Marzano, 2007, p. 1

Ensuring the highest quality mathematics education for every student requires effective teaching. In order to effectively teach mathematics, a teacher must possess:

- Knowledge of mathematical content and pedagogy

- Deep knowledge of the connections among mathematical ideas

- Thorough understanding of how students learn

- Knowledge of the school culture and expectations

The teaching of mathematics requires continual education and learning. To teach is a career-long endeavor. Thus, a highly effective mathematics education leader is skilled at supporting the growth of *every* teacher.

Principles and Standards for School Mathematics (NCTM, 2000) describes a vision of mathematics teaching and learning in which students are actively engaged in doing mathematics that allows them to identify the connections and relationships between the mathematics they have experienced and the mathematics they are learning. The development of closely allied mathematical skills and conceptual understandings is a direct result of the experiences teachers design and facilitate for students. Thus, successful learning of mathematics for every child requires much of the classroom teacher.

The revised edition of the National Council of Teachers of Mathematics' professional teaching standards in *Mathematics Teaching Today* (2007) argues that preK–12 teachers should be proficient in the following:

- "Designing and implementing mathematical experiences that stimulate students' interests and intellect;

- orchestrating classroom discourse in ways that promote the exploration and growth of mathematical ideas;

- using, and helping students use, technology and other tools to pursue mathematical investigations;

- assessing students' existing mathematical knowledge and challenging students to extend that knowledge;

- fostering positive attitudes about the aesthetic and utilitarian values of mathematics;

A highly effective mathematics education leader is skilled at supporting the growth of *every* teacher.

- engaging in opportunities to deepen their own understanding of the mathematics being studied and its applications;

- reflecting on the value of classroom encounters and taking action to improve their practice; and

- fostering professional and collegial relationships to enhance their own teaching performance." (pp. 5–6)

Given the social, political, and cultural contexts within which mathematics teaching occurs, a focus on success for every child is not easy. Yet implementation of research-informed practices and dedication to high-quality professional development and learning *for every teacher* establish the fundamental aspects of mathematics education leadership for teaching and learning.

Action Indicators for Teaching and Learning Leadership

The 21st-century mathematics leader seeks to ensure that students are provided with ample opportunity to engage in the five forms of mental activity that help students to build mathematical understanding, as identified by Carpenter and Lehrer (1999). They characterize understanding not as a static attribute but as emerging in student learners engaged in interrelated forms of learning:

1. Constructing relationships

2. Extending and applying mathematical knowledge

3. Reflecting about experiences

4. Articulating what one knows

5. Making mathematical knowledge one's own (Carpenter & Lehrer, 1999)

Developing understanding requires more than connecting new and prior knowledge; it requires a structuring of knowledge so that new knowledge can be "related to and incorporated into existing networks of knowledge rather than connected on an element-by-element basis" (Carpenter & Lehrer, 1999, p. 22).

In addition, mathematics must be taught in a way that develops mathematical skills and conceptual understanding simultaneously: "The integrated and balanced development of all five strands of mathematical proficiency (conceptual understanding, procedural fluency, strategic competence, adaptive reasoning, and productive dispositions) should guide the teaching and learning of school mathematics" (National Research Council, 2001, p. 21). To achieve this vision, the planning for instruction and instructional practices must align with well-articulated goals, instruction, and assessment. Students must be prepared to be active constructors of knowledge as required in today's workplace and advanced schooling.

A mathematics education leader ensures that teachers are experiencing continuous growth in their understanding of this type of mental activity and are actively searching for ways to provide students these types of experiences through

Mathematics must be taught in a way that develops mathematical skills and conceptual understanding simultaneously.

classroom lesson planning. The effective mathematics education leader needs to be knowledgeable of and promote research-informed teaching practices and effective instructional strategies. Remaining current in the mathematics education research and using that knowledge to provide for a high level of learning for every student are also required of each teacher, and will need to be taught and supported by the teacher leader. The leader must also determine how to integrate technology into the 21st-century mathematics classroom and then support its integration into the student learning experience.

Teaching and Learning Indicator 1

■ ■ ■ ■

Every teacher pursues the successful learning of mathematics for every student.

Stage 1 leaders will:

- Develop and model knowledge about instructional strategies for improved student learning.

- Identify student populations in need of additional support for success within the mathematics curriculum, and use strategies to meet the needs of those students.

Stage 2 leaders will:

- Engage teacher teams to collaboratively identify and implement common curricular outcomes.

- Engage teacher teams in the collaborative development and implementation of instructional strategies needed to support every learner.

- Ensure implementation of collaborative planning, common curriculum pacing, and improved instructional strategies by teacher teams.

Stage 3 leaders will:

- Ensure the implementation of a systemic plan for the continuous improvement of school, district, regional, or provincial student achievement across all populations.

- Monitor and respond to the level of attainment of targeted student achievement benchmarks, and publicly celebrate results with the extended school community.

Leadership of Self

Leadership of Others

Leadership in the Extended Community

High-performing collaborative teacher teams work together to identify the essential and valued student learning for each unit of study.

Stage 1: Know and Model

Stage 1 leaders pursue growth in their mathematical knowledge of differentiation and intervention strategies, and then actively integrate into practice and model newly acquired knowledge and strategies. The Stage 1 leader pursues and recognizes the importance of performance analysis for all student populations.

Ensuring the successful learning of mathematics requires an awareness of multiple perspectives on learning and teaching. It also requires an understanding of how to effectively help students interact with new knowledge and how to help students deepen their understanding of that knowledge. Identifying student populations in need of additional attention allows the leader to target those populations for interventions, support, challenge, recognition, and programs that meet individual needs as lessons are designed, modeled, and used by other colleagues.

Stage 2: Collaborate and Implement

The Stage 2 leader works collaboratively with teachers to ensure every student achieves his or her full learning potential. To accomplish this, high-performing collaborative teacher teams work together to identify the essential and valued student learning for each unit of study or course designed by the school, district, or province.

Judith Warren Little (1990) found that when teachers engage regularly in authentic joint work, focused on explicit, common learning goals, their collaboration pays off in the form of high-quality solutions to instructional problems, increased teacher confidence, and remarkable gains in student achievement. The Stage 2 leader ensures that:

- Teacher teams work together to develop effective lessons organized into cohesive units.

- Necessary professional development is provided so that teacher teams learn to develop a broad array of instructional strategies to differentiate, support, or challenge every student's learning.

- Common planning time and support are provided for teacher teams to analyze student achievement, share teaching strategies, identify specific learning outcomes, and create lessons that reflect team discussions.

Stage 3: Advocate and Systematize

Stage 3 leadership ensures school, district, state, or provincial implementation, monitoring, and modification of proactive interventions and support for student learning. Mathematical learning is supported through ongoing dialogue and cooperation among the students, teachers, parents, and support organizations outside the leader's daily arena of influence.

The Stage 3 leader analyzes the current status of student achievement on local and state assessments, ensures periodic review of common curricular outcomes, and leads the development of teacher craft knowledge regarding attainment of expected learning standards. Like the Stage 1 and Stage 2 leader, the Stage 3 leader celebrates improvement of student achievement results, but the Stage 3 leader celebrates improvement *publicly* to intentionally share with the extended school community both the results and the teacher actions that led to the improved results.

Teaching and Learning Indicator 2

■ ■ ■ ■

*Every teacher implements research-informed best practices
and uses effective instructional planning and
teaching strategies.*

Stage 1 leaders will:

- Develop and model knowledge of research-informed instructional strategies and best practices for effective student learning of mathematics.

- Formulate and implement effective lesson planning to achieve intended learning goals.

- Develop and model knowledge of tools necessary to assess the current status of teaching practices.

- Recognize the importance of technology integration into the mathematics curriculum.

Stage 2 leaders will:

- Determine the current status of teacher knowledge and implementation of research-informed, effective instructional strategies.

- Facilitate growth of teachers' mathematical knowledge and implementation of research-informed best practices.

- Engage teachers in collaborative dialogue about research-informed instructional practices and planning for effective student learning of mathematics.

- Collaborate with and support teachers in integrating technology into the mathematics curriculum.

Stage 3 leaders will:

- Ensure implementation of best-practice instruction in every student's learning experience throughout the district, region, or province.

- Facilitate a systemic continuous process of mathematics instructional improvement that reflects current research-informed practices.

- Ensure the ongoing use of technology as an embedded and systemic part of the mathematics curriculum and instruction at the district, regional, or provincial level.

Leadership of Self

Leadership of Others

*Leadership in the
Extended Community*

Collaborative teams ensure best-practice instruction is embedded in all classrooms.

Stage 1: Know and Model

Stage 1 leaders recognize that *teaching and learning* is the fundamental role of the school. This recognition compels the leader to learn more about research-informed strategies and then subsequently model best practices in the instructional classroom. The Stage 1 leader understands that lesson planning must provide opportunities for students to develop conceptual understanding, procedural fluency, adaptive reasoning, strategic competence, and productive dispositions. The importance of technology as a teaching and learning tool in mathematics is understood and used appropriately by the leader. The Stage 1 leader serves as a mentor and model of effective lesson design for other teachers and understands that excellent teaching leads to more precision and less prescription. As the Stage 1 leader investigates research into best practice, he or she also reflects upon action research in the local school setting as part of the analysis of "what works."

Stage 2: Collaborate and Implement

Stage 2 mathematics leaders become collaborators who share Stage 1 knowledge with teachers to help them develop a professional growth plan. The Stage 2 leader provides learning experiences that show teachers how to use research-informed strategies and practice. The leader realizes the importance of discourse, norms, and relationship-building as part of the experience, as teachers plan together for instruction and reflect on individual practice. The Stage 2 leader provides opportunities for teacher collaboration around the use of lesson study and other forms of professional learning related to effective lesson design.

Stage 3: Advocate and Systematize

The Stage 3 leader establishes a systemic process by which teaching practice and student learning must be improved throughout the school, district, region, or province. The process of integrating curriculum, instruction, and assessment into a systemic whole is used to drive program improvement. Collaborative teams of teachers are used as a tool throughout the district, region, or province in order to foster teacher-engaged learning and professional growth. These teams ensure best-practice instruction is embedded in all classrooms as evidence of student-engaged learning, effective teacher/student relationships, student interaction with new knowledge, and effective lesson design.

The Stage 3 leader contributes to and supports a more global discussion of action toward teacher reflection on practice and teacher demonstrations of classroom teaching. The Stage 3 leader ensures these discussions and actions include the various uses of technology to enhance differentiated instruction and connect meaningful and rigorous mathematics content to the student learner.

Teaching and Learning Indicator 3

■ ■ ■ □

Every teacher participates in continuous and meaningful mathematics professional development and learning in order to improve his or her practice.

Stage 1 leaders will:

- Develop and use knowledge regarding research-informed best practices in mathematics professional learning.

- Use current status of teachers' mathematical teaching and learning knowledge to identify areas for teacher improvement and growth.

- Engage in professional learning and reflection as a model of self-assessment and growth.

Stage 2 leaders will:

- Engage every teacher in appropriate professional learning and reflection regarding mathematics content, pedagogy, and assessment.

- Facilitate participation in collaborative site-based professional development and learning for every teacher.

Stage 3 leaders will:

- Implement a comprehensive professional development and learning plan for improved teacher growth and development throughout the district, region, or province.

- Ensure necessary resources, time within the school day, and support for continuous professional development and learning are provided to every teacher throughout the district, region, or province.

Leadership of Self

Leadership of Others

Leadership in the Extended Community

The leader understands the connection between adult learning theory and the continued professional growth of teachers.

Stage 1: Know and Model

A Stage 1 leader learns about effective professional development and learning and its inherent characteristics. The leader understands the connection between adult learning theory and the continued professional growth of teachers. The Stage 1 leader knows that intensive and sustained high-quality, content-based professional learning by teachers must reflect a well-defined vision of quality mathematics, effective classroom practices, and lesson planning. Mathematics teachers must have time to practice and reflect on various methods for teaching and representing mathematics content. The leader understands that teacher learning and improvement above all entail "learning to do the right things in the setting where you work" (Elmore, 2004, p. 73). The Stage 1 leader models to others the use of research-informed "right things" and uses them to assess the current status of each teacher's level of mathematical teaching and learning knowledge. Subsequently, in the context of the school workplace, the teacher uses research-informed practices as the Stage 1 basis for focused teacher growth and improvement.

Stage 2: Collaborate and Implement

The Stage 2 leader engages teachers and teacher teams in expanded professional development and learning discourse regarding mathematics pedagogy, mathematics content, and assessment. At this level, the leader recognizes the importance of continuous improvement for all teachers in these areas and acts accordingly; professional development and learning experiences are tied to teacher goals, research-informed best practices, and district needs.

Effective professional development and learning experiences, as indicated by Loucks-Horsley, Hewson, Love, & Stiles (1998) should:

- Be driven by a well-defined understanding of effective classroom learning and teaching.

- Provide opportunities for teachers to build their knowledge and skills collectively.

- Use or model with teachers the strategies teachers should use with their students.

- Build a learning community.

- Support teachers to serve in leadership roles.

- Ensure positive impact on teacher effectiveness, student learning, leadership, and the school community.

The Stage 2 mathematics education leader pursues these actions and recognizes that professional development and learning experiences must engage teachers in a collaborative setting, requiring teachers to work together as part of an ongoing professional learning experience.

Stage 3: Advocate and Systematize

The Stage 3 leader understands the importance of and uses an intentional, comprehensive teacher staff development plan that integrates growth in content knowledge, pedagogical knowledge, technological knowledge, and assessment skill throughout the district, region, or province—and implements such a plan.

The commitment of resources, dedicated time within the school day for teacher collaboration, and support for contextual and ongoing professional development and learning are essential for sustained, systemic change for the individual teacher, as well as various teacher teams. The Stage 3 leader seeks such commitments to this process from all of the educational stakeholders. The leader makes the commitment to share knowledge and address critical issues—such as time, equity, professional culture, leadership sustainability, and public support for the professional growth and learning of every mathematics teacher—and is committed to success regarding each of these issues.

The Stage 3 leader understands and acts upon the critical element of teacher growth, professional development, and learning taking place in the *context of the workplace.*

Curriculum Leadership

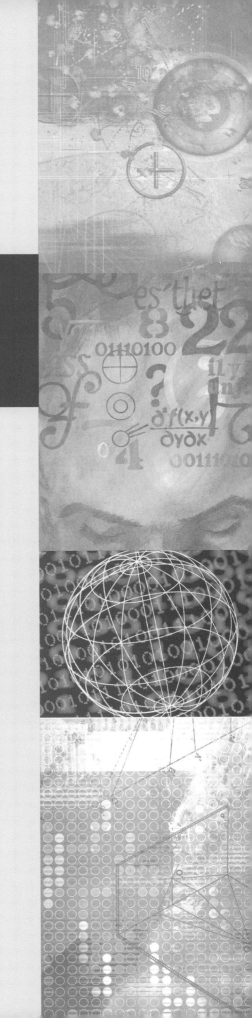

Principle 3:
Ensure relevant and meaningful mathematics in every lesson.

Indicator 1:

Every teacher implements the local curriculum and uses instructional resources that are coherent and reflect state standards and national curriculum recommendations.

Indicator 2:

Every teacher implements a curriculum that is focused on relevant and meaningful mathematics.

Indicator 3:

Every teacher implements the intended curriculum with needed intervention and makes certain it is attained by every student.

The NCSM Vision of Curriculum Leadership

The mathematics education leader ensures the curriculum is coherent, focused on important, relevant mathematics, and well articulated across the grades.

—National Council of Teachers of Mathematics, 2000, p. 3

A mathematics curriculum document is a developmental listing of knowledge and skills for which students should demonstrate mathematical competence. The following components should be included:

- A rationale that relates goals of mathematics to the school or district mission and vision

- A general description for the mathematical content

- Specific measurable learning indicators or objectives that are coherent and are organized to build on or connect to other ideas

- Alignment of the measurable learner objectives for each grade level or course to the knowledge, skills, and competencies students need to meet the school/district goals and state standards

- Instructional strategies, substantive lessons, and specific assessments with consistency in rigor

- Evidence that student learning objectives have been articulated by grade level/course sequence

The mathematics leader must lead collaborative efforts to develop coherent, meaningful curriculum that encourage the teaching of higher levels of mathematics and advanced skills. The mathematics curriculum leader helps define what students are expected to know and be able to do; leads teachers in creating coherence and connectedness of prioritized indicators to state standards as well as national curriculum recommendations; and guarantees the curriculum focuses on mathematical content that every student must learn, including numbers and operations, algebra, geometry, measurement, probability, data analysis/statistics, and discrete mathematics.

Curriculum Focal Points for PreKindergarten Through 8th Grade Mathematics (2006) provides guidance on how to design a rigorous and coherent curriculum. According to NCTM (2000), the mathematics curriculum should:

- Be meaningful.

- Promote high standards.

- Be focused on important mathematics.

- Have measurable goals.

- Be built around key concepts and understandings.

> The mathematics leader must lead collaborative efforts to develop coherent, meaningful curriculum that encourage the teaching of higher levels of mathematics and advanced skills.

- Contain focused, relevant mathematics designed to prepare students to think critically in problem-solving environments.

- Prepare students for further mathematics studies in a variety of settings.

The curriculum leader engages in a coordinated articulation process, spanning grades preK–12, to determine the current status and subsequent gaps in the intended curriculum, the implemented curriculum, and the attained curriculum. The *intended* curriculum is the written guide of the standards, goals, and indicators and objectives that must be addressed at each grade level and in each course. The intended curriculum is aligned with school and state assessments and identifies essential outcomes for every learner to acquire and the enrichment or supplementary material to be studied if time permits. The *implemented* curriculum refers to the actual content taught by the teacher as well as the intentional intervention and support provided to the students at risk of not attaining the learning goals. The *attained* curriculum refers to the actual content learned by every student.

Action Indicators for Curriculum Leadership

Growth in curriculum leadership reflects a clear understanding of how to bridge the gap between the intended district curriculum and the actual implemented classroom curriculum. The process of successful curriculum implementation, while complex, is vital. Leadership of the curriculum in mathematics also requires the leader to provide a clear path that ensures the *intended* curriculum is implemented and subsequently is the *learned* curriculum for every child.

Curriculum Indicator 1

■ ■ ■ ■

Every teacher implements the local curriculum and uses instructional resources that are coherent and reflect state standards and national curriculum recommendations.

Leadership of Self

Leadership of Others

Leadership in the Extended Community

Stage 1 leaders will:

- Develop and apply knowledge of state standards and national curriculum recommendations and their impact on the local curriculum.

- Recognize, understand, and model the connection between the coherence and focus of the local curriculum to effective instruction and achievement.

Stage 2 leaders will:

- Engage teachers and collaboratively develop local curriculum consistent with state standards.

- Ensure coherent and consistent implementation of the local curriculum by all teachers.

Stage 3 leaders will:

- Ensure coherent implementation and ongoing review by district, regional, or provincial stakeholders for the alignment of local curriculum with state and national curriculum recommendations and assessments.

Stage 1: Know and Model

The Stage 1 mathematics leader recognizes the *curriculum* as the school or district document that translates national curriculum recommendations and state and local standards into an organized developmental list of learning objectives, with accompanying materials for student use (program, text, other resources), and lesson designs for use by teachers. The Stage 1 leader uses curriculum that reflect state standards, assists teachers and students in identifying mathematics concepts, and provides well-designed lessons, including supplementary materials for intervention and support of student learning.

The extent to which a curriculum addresses all of the aforementioned will determine the underlying strength of the curriculum. A leader at this stage becomes knowledgeable about NCTM's *Principles and Standards for School Mathematics* (2000) and *Curriculum Focal Points* (2006), as well as other materials and programs that support student learning of high standards—and acts to teach and model that knowledge.

Stage 2: Collaborate and Implement

At Stage 2, the leader collaborates with teachers and teacher teams to begin the alignment and connections process. Learning goals for all students are matched to national curriculum recommendations and state goals. The leader ensures that the district organizes teaching and learning based upon the idea that every student can achieve learning goals at high levels.

The mathematics leader must work collaboratively with other teachers and mathematics leaders to examine the preK–12 grade mathematics curriculum for coherence and articulation across all grade levels. The curriculum must be designed to incorporate prior learning and should provide a coherent and connected structure that is developmentally appropriate from grade level to grade level. Content should be presented to students when they are cognitively capable of understanding specific concepts and can see relationships among ideas.

The Stage 2 leader ensures the intended curriculum is implemented by all teachers and teacher teams.

A coherent curriculum effectively organizes and integrates important mathematical ideas so that concepts can build and connect. The Stage 2 leader ensures all teachers collaborate to create and implement an articulated curriculum that shows connections between lessons, grade levels, and courses. These connections make possible an increasingly rigorous development of ideas. Since an articulated curriculum includes directions for introducing, extending, and formalizing what has been taught previously, with emphasis on the connections among related topics, the leader teaches and develops this knowledge among all teachers and local community stakeholders. The Stage 2 leader ensures the intended curriculum is implemented by all teachers and teacher teams and that the curriculum presents rigorous opportunities for students to push their thinking beyond core expectations.

Stage 3: Advocate and Systematize

A Stage 3 leader maintains continuous improvement of a curriculum aligned to national curriculum recommendations and state standards. The leader continually assesses and modifies the local mathematics curriculum in collaboration with others and seeks to influence and be influenced beyond the local arena. The mathematics leader plans and provides ongoing opportunities for district, regional, or provincial curriculum revision. The Stage 3 leader ensures the curriculum is refined and clarified every 3 to 5 years by a variety of district, regional, or provincial stakeholders to reflect current research findings.

The Stage 3 leader ensures an ongoing process that enables and supports teachers to implement a relevant, rigorous, and meaningful mathematics curriculum for every student. This process requires the leadership and commitment of the mathematics leader, as well as the involvement of all teachers. Curriculum planning, vision, and revision are key elements to building a coherent and articulated mathematics curriculum that promotes equitable learning opportunities and holds all students to high standards of achievement.

Curriculum Indicator 2

■ ■ ■ ■

Every teacher implements a curriculum that is focused on relevant and meaningful mathematics.

Stage 1 leaders will:

- Develop awareness of, understand, and model the rationale, characteristics, and qualities of meaningful, relevant, and important mathematics.

- Develop an awareness of and model the applications and connections within mathematics and other content areas.

Stage 2 leaders will:

- Engage teachers and teacher teams in developing and implementing meaningful and relevant mathematics curriculum for each course or grade level.

Stage 3 leaders will:

- Ensure the collective analysis and continuous systemic improvement of the implemented local curriculum throughout the district, region, or province.

Leadership of Self

Leadership of Others

Leadership in the Extended Community

Stage 1: Know and Model

The Stage 1 leader becomes knowledgeable about NCTM's connections, communication, and reasoning standards from *Principles and Standards for School Mathematics* (2000) and models these standards for others. The Stage 1 leader understands and models how attention to mathematical connections and applications affects the way mathematics is taught at all levels.

The Stage 1 leader understands the curriculum must deliver meaningful and important mathematics presented in ways and with contexts that are responsive to cultural diversity. Important, relevant mathematics content helps in developing other mathematical ideas, connecting areas of mathematics, and in representing and solving problems within or outside of mathematics. NCTM (2000) suggests that foundational concepts such as number systems and algebraic structures, mathematical equivalence, the study of change including proportionality, function, and rate of change, the study of shape, and the study of chance must be a major focus of the curriculum. These topics and others enable students to understand mathematical ideas as well as to connect ideas across different areas of mathematics. Important, relevant mathematics topics may change over time, and the leader maintains an awareness and model of these changes for others.

Stage 2: Collaborate and Implement

The Stage 2 leader collaborates with and supports teachers and teacher teams to ensure they are developing and implementing a meaningful and relevant mathematics curriculum for all students. The leader ensures that teachers and teacher teams enrich the mathematics curriculum to address mathematical connections and applications. Stage 2 leaders help teachers develop a mathematics curriculum that prepares students to solve problems in school, home, and work settings. The Stage 2 leader becomes a teacher of these expectations for curriculum implementation. The leader provides teachers and teacher teams with resources and professional development and learning opportunities that support curriculum-based best practices. The Stage 2 leader ensures the curriculum focuses on relevant and meaningful mathematics and establishes ongoing teacher and teacher-team curriculum review and accountability for this purpose.

Stage 3: Advocate and Systematize

The Stage 3 leader must stay abreast of current developments in post-secondary education and the workforce, knowing how and when mathematical concepts, connections, and applications are used. The Stage 3 leader seeks to impact the district, regional, or provincial mathematics curriculum and ensures it is updated on an ongoing basis to reflect current practices and research. The leader provides the energy behind an ongoing and systemic analysis of the local implemented curriculum and targets specific grade levels or courses for annual improvement. The Stage 3 leader also maintains and ensures that meaningful and relevant mathematics curriculum are implemented by every teacher throughout the district, region, or province. The Stage 3 leader becomes intentional about teaching and leading the development and understanding of a relevant and meaningful curriculum among and with an expanded community of educational stakeholders.

Curriculum Indicator 3

■ ■ ■ ■

Every teacher implements the intended curriculum with needed intervention and makes certain it is attained by every student.

Stage 1 leaders will:

- Examine and model the congruence among the intended curriculum, the implemented curriculum, and the attained curriculum.

Stage 2 leaders will:

- Engage teachers and teacher teams in identifying and acting on inconsistencies among the intended, implemented, and attained curriculum.

- Engage teachers and teacher teams in developing and implementing vertically aligned curriculum.

Stage 3 leaders will:

- Ensure congruence between the developed and implemented curriculum throughout the district, regional, or provincial mathematics programs.

- Participate in the systemic development, implementation, and student attainment of a well-articulated, rigorous, and coherent preK–12 mathematics curriculum throughout the district, region, or province.

Leadership of Self

Leadership of Others

Leadership in the Extended Community

The intended curriculum must be implemented by *every* teacher.

Stage 1: Know and Model

The Stage 1 leader must determine if the curriculum is aligned in order to provide the opportunity for each student to learn. It is crucial the leader guarantee curriculum implementation by providing teachers and teacher teams clear guidance about the curriculum to be delivered at each grade level and in each course. Vertical and horizontal alignments are important components of a viable curriculum. Vertical alignment ensures a smooth, well-sequenced flow of content that develops appropriate student skills from one grade or course to the next, resulting in few gaps and avoiding needless repetition. Horizontal alignment ensures consistency within grade levels or courses, guaranteeing comparable learning outcomes and levels of rigor for each grade level or course. It is entirely possible that methods incorporated by each teacher may vary, but the *expected outcomes* and *pacing* must be constant. The intended curriculum must be implemented by *every* teacher. Thus, the Stage 1 leader provides a model for ensuring the implementation of the expected and intended curriculum.

The Stage 1 leader also must analyze student achievement data to measure whether the implemented curriculum was attained. The Stage 1 leader then uses the data to support the need for an alignment process, beginning with recording and reviewing the taught curriculum. This process reveals the extent to which the content that is taught matches the written and tested curriculum. A schoolwide review identifies inconsistencies, gaps, redundancies, and integration opportunities. After the implemented curriculum is reviewed by the Stage 1 leader, revisions can be made based upon identified student needs.

Stage 2: Collaborate and Implement

At Stage 2, the mathematics leader initiates and facilitates collaborative teacher team discussions and actions about curriculum standards to ensure they are clearly articulated across all levels to eliminate gaps and overlaps. The leader engages teachers and teacher teams in developing a vertically and horizontally aligned mathematics curriculum. To achieve coherence and articulation, the curriculum focuses on concepts and skills that are critical to the understanding of important processes and concepts developed over several age levels. The leader engages teacher teams in discussions and actions that will *eliminate disparities and rigor inconsistencies* among the intended curriculum, the implemented curriculum, and the attained curriculum, and ensures all teachers focus on the disparities.

The Stage 2 leader engages teachers and teacher teams in actions that develop and implement curriculum guides to plan the pacing of instruction and assessment. Finally, the Stage 2 leader ensures teachers and teacher teams identify and address inconsistencies, gaps, and redundancies revealed by student achievement data between the implemented and attained curriculum.

Stage 3: Advocate and Systematize

The Stage 3 leader monitors the implementation of the intended curriculum at the district, regional, or provincial level. A combination of student achievement data (the attained curriculum), classroom observations (the implemented curriculum), and professional conversations around the intended curriculum provides a rich picture of the level of implementation of the curriculum across departments, grade levels, schools, or regions. All the data together can be compiled and used to help establish professional development plans as well as staff development and learning opportunities for a wide variety of educational stakeholders.

The Stage 3 leader should actively translate the importance of effective curriculum practices and conduct regular curriculum review meetings with administrators, parents, and the community at large. Moreover, the Stage 3 leader becomes an expert at interpreting local, state, regional, or provincial assessment data to locate and act upon the gaps between the intended and attained curriculum within and among all student populations.

Assessment Leadership

Principle 4:

Ensure timely, accurate monitoring of student learning and adjustment of teacher instruction for improved student learning.

Indicator 1:

Every teacher uses student assessments that are congruent and aligned by grade level or course content.

Indicator 2:

Every teacher uses formative assessment processes to inform teacher practice and student learning.

Indicator 3:

Every teacher uses summative assessment data to evaluate mathematics grade level, course, and program effectiveness.

The NCSM Vision of Assessment Leadership

The teaching profession is a calling, a calling with the potential to do enormous good for students. Although we haven't traditionally seen it in this light, assessment plays an indispensable role in fulfilling our calling. Used with skill, assessment can motivate the unmotivated, restore the desire to learn, and encourage students to keep learning, and it can actually create—not simply measure—increased achievement.

—Stiggins, Arter, Chappuis, & Chappuis, 2006, p. 3

Assessment is the multifaceted process by which we gather information about students, teachers, schools, and districts to inform our decision-making, adjust our instruction, and revise our curriculum. Effective assessment is grounded in the ongoing retrieval and analysis of information about the quality and quantity of student learning. As such, assessment connects the components of a mathematics program (alignment), informs ongoing instruction (formative assessment), and provides insights into the degree of success of the overall program (summative assessment).

Too often, however, assessment is limited to summative tests and high-stakes assessments that assign grades, scores, and rankings without the expectation, or often even the capacity, to use this information to make improvements and adjustments. Too often, what is tested is tightly aligned with neither what is taught, nor how it is taught. Too often, classroom instruction fails to take advantage of the wealth of formative information that can, and must, be gathered during every lesson. Too often, decisions are made, sometimes with serious consequences, on the basis of unreliable information or without attention to available data.

These missed opportunities can be prevented when our conception of learning balances assessment *for* learning (used for making instructional decisions and monitoring student progress) with assessment *of* learning (used for evaluating students' achievement and evaluating programs). The form and content of our assessment must match the form and content of instruction. Our understanding of assessment must change from seeing it as mere after-the-fact testing to using it as an integral component of the planning-teaching-assessing cycle that characterizes high-quality instruction.

NCSM's vision for assessment goes beyond mastering the dual purposes of formative and summative assessment. A mathematics education leader must adopt a broader view of the purposes and roles of assessment. The leader must understand the importance of gathering and interpreting relevant assessment data that contribute meaningful feedback for students, teachers, and administrators—all in the service of improving student achievement for each and every student.

This is possible when:

- The mathematics that is taught, the way it is taught, and how it is assessed are deliberately and coherently aligned.

NCSM's vision for assessment goes beyond mastering the dual purposes of formative and summative assessment. A mathematics education leader must adopt a broader view of the purposes and roles of assessment.

- Students' answers, solutions, errors, questions, explanations, body language, homework, quizzes, and tests are seen as components of the formative assessment data used to make decisions about moving forward, re-teaching, intervening, and addressing individual and small-group needs.

- Summative assessments are collaboratively designed and coherently aligned with learning goals.

- The student work that emerges from these assessments is carefully analyzed to make decisions about how and where improvements must be made.

Although research on various aspects of assessment is still in its infancy, we do know the following:

- Children who have the opportunity to learn the content on which they will be assessed score higher than children who do not learn the content before they are assessed (Conzemius & O'Neill, 2001).

- In successful schools, there is a strong focus on aligning the curriculum with classroom assessments (Chrispeels, Strait, & Brown, 1999).

- Analysis of student data, along with focused planning, also leads to improvement of student achievement (Teddlie & Stringfield, 1993).

Thus, leaders must fully understand and act upon the multiple purposes of assessment. They must be astute at planning and developing assessments, gathering assessment data, analyzing and interpreting the data, and communicating the results of this analysis to other adults. As a result of this process, leaders connect "How did we do?" to "How can we do better?"

Finally, assessment is not just a means to measure how well students are learning or how effectively teachers are teaching. It is also the primary means by which leaders quantitatively and qualitatively judge their *own* effectiveness. The multifaceted process of assessment provides the basis for leadership accountability and effectiveness when mathematics education leaders are held responsible for creating the conditions by which teachers can most effectively generate high levels of learning for every student.

Action Indicators for Assessment Leadership

Assessment cannot function solely as an accountability measure. Effective leaders recognize the skillful use of assessment can work in positive ways to benefit teacher and student learning.

Assessment *for* learning occurs when teams of teachers use classroom assessment and other information sources about student achievement in order to advance student learning. According to the Assessment Training Institute, outstanding assessment actions include teachers, leaders, and teacher teams that:

- Understand and articulate *in advance of teaching* the achievement targets for students.

> Leaders connect "How did we do?" to "How can we do better?"

- Become assessment literate so they can transform those expectations into assessment exercises and scoring procedures that *accurately reflect student achievement.*

- Use classroom assessments *to build student confidence* in themselves as learners, helping students take responsibility for their own learning so as to lay a foundation for lifelong learning.

- Translate classroom assessment results into *frequent, descriptive (versus judgmental)* feedback for students, providing them with specific insights regarding their strengths as well as how to improve.

- *Adjust instruction* continuously based on the results of classroom assessments.

- *Involve students in actively communicating* with their teachers and their families about their achievement status and improvement.

- Make sure that students understand *how the achievement targets* they strive to achieve now *relate to those that will come after.* (Stiggins, 2002, p. 762)

The described teacher "assessment actions" build a bridge across the barrier belief that assessment is solely about measurement. As leaders adopt more productive beliefs about using assessments to promote learning, teachers and teacher teams will be more able to identify areas of personal improvement as well as improvement in overall mathematics program quality—aligned across grades and courses.

This effort will, in turn, result in erasing the inequities caused by the wide application of assessment as a private teacher act solely for the purpose of assigning grades.

Assessment Indicator 1

■ ■ ■ ■

Every teacher uses student assessments that are congruent and aligned by grade level or course content.

Stage 1 leaders will:

- Ensure assessment measures important mathematics— mathematics that is relevant and serves as critical underpinning for future learning.

- Recognize and model the importance of aligning content expectations and instructional practices with the form and content of assessment.

- Recognize and model a response to inequities created by inconsistent assessment instruments and inappropriate grading practices.

Stage 2 leaders will:

- Ensure teachers provide students the opportunity to learn the mathematics to be assessed.

- Collaboratively ensure alignment between school and district assessments with state standards and national curriculum recommendations.

- Participate in and lead teams in school- and district-level development of common assessments and scoring rubrics to ensure alignment with instructional practice.

Stage 3 leaders will:

- Engage in the periodic review and updating of local, regional, or provincial assessments to respond to changing conditions and insights gained from prior assessment.

- Provide teachers, teacher teams, and administrators with requisite professional development and learning about assessment literacy.

- Facilitate and conduct effective public dialogue about the role, process, development, and results of assessments with all stakeholders at the district, regional, or provincial level.

Leadership of Self

Leadership of Others

Leadership in the Extended Community

Stage 1: Know and Model

Stage 1 leaders are aware of national and state trends and mandates for assessment. The leader is aware of the need to receive feedback about assessment data and ensures mathematics assessments are measuring important mathematics that are aligned from grade level to grade level and course to course.

Student assessments must have consistent levels of rigor across teachers. The Stage 1 leader addresses inequities in the rigor of his or her own assessments compared to the assessments of other grade- or course-level teachers. The Stage 1 leader knows, understands, and models appropriate assessment instruments and grading practices, including the use of technology. The Stage 1 leader also models the appropriate communication between students and parents regarding the expectations of assessments and the necessary student preparation for those assessments.

Stage 2: Collaborate and Implement

Stage 2 leaders engage teachers and teacher teams in collaborative discussions regarding local assessment alignment with state standards and national curriculum recommendations. The leader helps teacher teams to construct both the assessments—which reflect consistent rigor in design—and the scoring rubrics used to grade the assessments, to ensure consistency in how student achievement is reported. The Stage 2 leader also supports communication among students, teachers, and parents about what mathematical content will be assessed, and how it will be assessed.

For the Stage 2 leader, the hardest aspect of assessment reform is not setting the standards or developing tests, but rather translating those standards and formative assessments into real changes in curriculum, instruction, and learning opportunities. The Stage 2 leader becomes expert at leading team implementation of the identified changes as part of an ongoing process.

Stage 3: Advocate and Systematize

Stage 3 leaders analyze the current status of the district assessment system to ensure alignment between local and state assessments of essential mathematics content throughout all grades and courses. The Stage 3 leader ensures that well-defined learning targets are a systemic part of assessment in the mathematics program. The Stage 3 leader provides professional development and learning regarding assessment literacy at the district, regional, or provincial level and conducts public discussions regarding the effective use of assessment.

Assessment Indicator 2

■ ■ ■ ■

Every teacher uses formative assessment processes to inform teacher practice and student learning.

Stage 1 leaders will:

- Use multiple sources of student assessment data to help teachers inform and improve their teaching practice.

- Learn and model the use of formative assessment and its impact on student learning.

- Recognize and model the importance of ongoing student feedback as a part of the student learning process.

Stage 2 leaders will:

- Assist teachers and teacher teams in developing and implementing formative assessments that will optimize opportunities for every student to learn.

- Facilitate effective teacher dialogue and interdependent practice regarding the implementation of formative assessment and ongoing student feedback.

Stage 3 leaders will:

- Create and support structures that allow teams of teachers at the district, regional, or provincial level to collectively analyze assessment data to enhance student learning.

- Develop and monitor a systemic district, regional, or provincial process through which teachers provide students with timely, ongoing, and meaningful feedback.

- Inform administrators, parents, and the education community of assessment results from multiple sources of data.

Leadership of Self

Leadership of Others

Leadership in the Extended Community

Stage 1: Know and Model

Stage 1 leaders understand the tenets of assessment *for* learning and the power of formative assessments as a means rather than an end to learning. The Stage 1 leader develops and models assessment literacy; the leader knows how to use classroom assessment as a teaching tool to motivate students to strive for higher levels of learning and to motivate other teachers to strive for higher levels of student achievement.

The leader models the assessment process and helps teachers match various types of formative assessment to particular kinds of knowledge and skills. The leader uses questioning strategies that challenge every student to reveal reasoning, think more deeply, and support conclusions with data.

Stage 2: Collaborate and Implement

Stage 2 leaders engage teachers and teacher teams in collaborative discussion to ensure grading practices provide students with opportunities to learn from formative assessments. The Stage 2 leader provides the support and time necessary for teachers and teacher teams to create and use a variety of formative assessment sources, including in-class techniques such as electronic SMART boards, "explain your thinking," small-groups problem-solving, and small-group discourse questioning. Nontraditional assessment alternatives such as performance-based, project-based, or language-based assessments are taught by the leader as well.

The leader also ensures teachers and teacher teams use formative data to improve student learning through ongoing student feedback. The leader uses multiple sources of student assessment data to inform student practice and ensures that teachers and teacher teams collectively examine classroom assessment information. Teams use the information on an ongoing basis to revise and guide teaching and learning as well as to ensure consistent levels of rigor.

Stage 3: Advocate and Systematize

Stage 3 leaders ensure that Stage 2 actions are fulfilled as part of an ongoing systemic assessment process culture at the district, regional, or provincial level.

Quality formative assessment is not an event. It is a process through which teachers and teacher teams work together to provide students with meaningful feedback on performance, to analyze congruent assessment data in order to enhance student learning, and to use student assessment results across all grades and courses to inform teacher practice in mathematics. When a formative assessment identifies students who are not successful, the Stage 3 leader implements a variety of interventions and supports for those students.

The Stage 3 leader is adept at informing school and district administrators and parents about formative assessment results and how these affect student achievement growth and student course taking patterns over time. The Stage 3 leader also shares the formative assessment process and its intended impact on student learning with the expanded educational community.

Assessment Indicator 3

■ ■ ■ ■

Every teacher uses summative assessment data to evaluate mathematics grade-level, course, and program effectiveness throughout a district, region, or province.

Stage 1 leaders will:

- Develop and model an understanding of summative assessment and its impact on student learning.

- Ensure all assessments are constructed to maximize the likelihood students can demonstrate the mathematics they know.

- Recognize and model the importance of ongoing student feedback as a part of the student learning process.

Stage 2 leaders will:

- Engage teachers and teacher teams in meaningful dialogue about large-scale local, state, and national assessment data and how to use the data to inform practice.

- Assist teachers and teacher teams in developing and implementing summative assessments that will optimize opportunities for every student to learn.

- Engage teachers in collaborative discussions regarding the use of summative assessment data to improve student learning.

Stage 3 leaders will:

- Facilitate use of local, state, and national summative assessment data in evaluating the continuous improvement and effectiveness of the local mathematics program.

- Implement and monitor a systemic process to ensure that all summative assessments are fair and free of bias at the district, regional, or provincial level.

- Inform administrators, parents, and the extended education community of assessment results from multiple sources of data.

Leadership of Self

Leadership of Others

Leadership in the Extended Community

Stage 1: Know and Model

Stage 1 leaders understand and model the purpose and power of summative assessments. They do the following:

- Identify and investigate methods for evaluating overall mathematics program improvement.

- Use trend data to determine school or district levels of long-term effectiveness and improvement.

- Examine data reflecting student achievement across all populations, as well as student access to the core mathematics curriculum preK–12.

The Stage 1 leader reports findings from summative assessments to students, parents, and teachers; provides meaningful and ongoing feedback to students; and subsequently targets areas of student and program improvement. The Stage 1 leader also ensures that the tested curriculum is aligned with the implemented curriculum.

Stage 2: Collaborate and Implement

Stage 2 leaders use data to engage teacher teams in grade-level or course improvement discussions, and they support the identification of weaknesses that need to be addressed. The Stage 2 leader engages teachers in discussion to build consensus on the use of summative data to improve student learning through adjustments in the mathematics program—and expects teachers to act on those discussions. The leader uses multiple sources of student summative assessment data to inform student practice and helps teachers to collectively and correctly use classroom assessment information to revise and guide the teaching and learning throughout the mathematics program. The Stage 2 leader inspects gaps in the learned curriculum based on demonstrations of student performance and the implemented curriculum. The leader helps teacher teams close gaps through revised instruction and assessment.

Stage 3: Advocate and Systematize

Stage 3 leaders ensure the use of summative data—assessment *of* learning—as an integral part of each teacher and teacher team's assessment literacy. The leader embeds some assessment items that mimic the form of district and state tests on other assessments and in instruction to help students gain facility with different types of items. The leader ensures that short-term and long-term assessment goals are established throughout the school/district and celebrates advancement toward those goals. The leader examines all levels of assessments to determine if they are fair and free of bias and subsequently provides assessment literacy staff development and learning for teachers as needed. The Stage 3 leader communicates expertly to administrators, parents, and the extended educational community on the meaning and implications of summative data and mathematics programmatic issues. He or she shows stakeholders how these affect decisions regarding housing patterns, industry growth, and pathways to higher education. Moreover, the Stage 3 leader becomes expert at understanding best-practice assessment reform and seeks to impact the regional, provincial, or national movement toward the use of summative assessments in local districts.

Becoming a PRIME Leader

One thing is clear about the stages of systemic school improvement efforts—a body of expert knowledge is required to carry them off.

—Elmore, 2007, p. 32

The PRIME Leadership Principles in Action

The PRIME Leadership Framework describes four principles, each with three specific indicators that together represent the state of conditions that needs to exist in our schools if every student is to experience improved achievement in mathematics. The trending toward these conditions is dependent upon the expert knowledge development of the mathematics education leader. As Richard Elmore (2007) explains in *Let's Act Like Professionals*, this knowledge will be partly technical (instructional expertise and the accompanying knowledge of practice that promotes adult learning), partly managerial (knowledge about organizational design and resource allocations), and partly sociopolitical (knowledge about how to make the institutional connections necessary to sustain an improvement strategy over time).

Thus, the PRIME Leadership Framework calls on mathematics education leaders to advance our technical, managerial, and sociopolitical knowledge as well as the knowledge of those we lead. PRIME leaders will create working and teaching conditions that will do the following:

- Address gaps in mathematics achievement expectations and access for all student populations.

- Require pursuit of meaningful, relevant, diverse, rigorous, and successful mathematics experiences for every child.

- Require alignment, coherence, and congruence to the curriculum and assessment of the curriculum.

- Sustain the collaborative discussion and use of aligned formative and summative assessments necessary to inform teaching and learning.

These adult leadership actions provide the focus for the knowledge and skills growth leaders must pursue.

Ultimately, a PRIME leader seeks to discover and fulfill his or her leadership potential. The PRIME leader seeks continuous growth as new knowledge of best practice emerges from research and practice. Mathematics programs will only get better when leaders open themselves and other teachers to new ideas, risk imaginatively, and enthusiastically inspire those they lead with a desire to learn and grow together. It is the PRIME leader who will close the "knowing-doing" gap between our knowledge about how to enhance student achievement and the commitment to actions we must take as a result of that knowledge.

As has been noted, student achievement is unlikely to advance much beyond current levels unless mathematics education leaders convert the indicators into a daily reality and exercise professional responsibility and accountability for their own practice and the practice of those teachers they lead. When leaders pursue teacher collaboration and view learning together as a professional obligation, this vision of success for every student can become a reality.

> It is the PRIME leader who will close the "knowing-doing" gap between our knowledge about how to enhance student achievement and the commitment to actions we must take as a result of that knowledge.

The stages of PRIME leadership growth provide a template for the expert knowledge and actions needed to lead others toward this vision. For NCSM members, and all those leading mathematics education improvement efforts, the PRIME Framework can guide our intentional leadership efforts: "Leadership is about learning that leads to constructive change" (Lambert, 1998, p. 9). Mathematics teachers cannot significantly improve their craft in isolation from others. Adult teaching and student learning improve when leaders create "formats, structures, [and cultures for collaborative discussions] that reflect change and assess current practice" (Glickman, 2002, p. 4). The PRIME principles provide the first steps in leading others to become engaged and committed professional mathematics education leaders.

The PRIME leader also understands that the technical and analytical skills described in the PRIME document will not be sufficient. Using extensive research, Goleman and colleagues (2002) assert that relational skills account for nearly three times as much impact on organizational change and performance as do analytical skills. Relational leaders:

- Listen to their colleagues without interrupting or judging.

- Respect confidences, never betraying a secret or private conversation.

- Practice empathy through deliberate inquiry.

The PRIME leader understands that sincere passion for the mission described in this document must be exhibited every day with genuine concern and interest for those he or she leads. Research shows that "in organizations of all types, both public and private, large and small, for-profit and nonprofit, relationships—particularly with leaders—are one of the single greatest predictors of employee performance, satisfaction and turnover" (Buckingham & Coffman, 1999 as cited in Reeves, 2006, p. 42). Thus, the capacity building of positive relationships with others must become an intentional pursuit of a PRIME leader.

The PRIME indicators and actions are also intended as a framework for reflection and self-assessment. Reflections on leadership practice should be an individual and a collective practice stimulated by discussion with others. Veteran leaders should model reflective practices for novice leaders. Structured conversations around the stages for each leadership indicator provide an intentional focus for which areas of leadership would be most important for short and long-term focus. It would be expected that every leader eventually pursues Stage 2 leadership, and if appropriate to job or career expectations, moves into Stage 3.

The PRIME Leadership Framework describes the "what" leaders are to pursue and become. The next question will be "how." How will we achieve the various indicators and stages for mathematics education leadership? These answers will be provided by our collective intuitive and research-informed understanding of what really works and by our teaching and learning from one another. We must dedicate ourselves to learning together on how to deliver and live the core

The PRIME principles provide the first steps in leading others to become engaged and committed professional mathematics education leaders.

values of equity, teaching and learning, curriculum, and assessment described in PRIME. The benefactors of this pursuit—our teachers and our students—are counting on it.

In the opening epigraph to this document on page iii, Kouzes and Posner remind us that "a leader's legacy is the legacy of many." Ultimately, the success of a mathematics education leader resides in the impact the leader leaves on the next generation of mathematics education leaders and programs. When leaders decide to *make a difference*, they choose to take a stand and commit themselves and others to a complex, yet crystal-clear set of leadership actions. PRIME describes those actions upon which each leader must take a stand. Every leader is capable of making commitments on things that matter and giving meaning to values that will significantly impact student learning. This is what it means to live a courageous leadership life. This is what it means to *be* a PRIME leader.

The PRIME Leadership Framework

Principle	Indicator 1	Indicator 2	Indicator 3
Equity Leadership	Every teacher addresses gaps in mathematics achievement expectations for all student populations.	Every teacher provides each student access to relevant and meaningful mathematics experiences.	Every teacher works interdependently in a collaborative learning community to erase inequities in student learning.
Teaching and Learning Leadership	Every teacher pursues the successful learning of mathematics for every student.	Every teacher implements research-informed best practices and uses effective instructional planning and teaching strategies.	Every teacher participates in continuous and meaningful mathematics professional development and learning in order to improve his or her practice.
Curriculum Leadership	Every teacher implements the local curriculum and uses instructional resources that are coherent and reflect state standards and national curriculum recommendations.	Every teacher implements a curriculum that is focused on relevant and meaningful mathematics.	Every teacher implements the intended curriculum with needed intervention and makes certain it is attained by every student.
Assessment Leadership	Every teacher uses student assessments that are congruent and aligned by grade level or course content.	Every teacher uses formative assessment processes to inform teacher practice and student learning.	Every teacher uses summative assessment data to evaluate mathematics grade-level, course, and program effectiveness.

Equity Leadership

Principle 1: Ensure high expectations and access to meaningful mathematics learning for every student.

Indicator	Stage 1 Leaders	Stage 2 Leaders	Stage 3 Leaders
1. Every teacher addresses gaps in mathematics achievement expectations for all student populations.	• Identify and analyze student achievement data for various populations. • Develop and apply knowledge about how to meet the diverse needs of all student populations. • Provide specific attention to those students farthest from expected standards of rigor and achievement.	• Engage teacher teams to collaboratively establish targeted benchmarks for improved student performance in each area of the mathematics program. • Engage grade-level and course-based teacher teams in a process of analyzing student achievement data in order to monitor student achievement across all populations.	• Ensure the implementation of a systemic plan for the continuous improvement of student achievement across all populations throughout the district, region, or province. • Monitor the level of attainment of targeted benchmarks, use analysis of results to inform and improve practice, and publicly celebrate successful results with the extended school community.
2. Every teacher provides each student access to relevant and meaningful mathematics experiences.	• Develop, model, and apply knowledge and strategies that reflect the importance of connecting mathematics to the context of students' experiences. • Identify patterns of student access to the mathematics curriculum.	• Engage teachers in the development and implementation of lessons that reflect the importance of relevant, meaningful mathematics. • Engage teachers to create and implement strategies that improve student access to the mathematics curriculum, and ensure teachers act on those strategies.	• Ensure the school, district, regional, or provincial mathematics program is vertically and horizontally aligned and reflects relevant and meaningful content. • Ensure implementation of school, district, regional, or provincial policy and practice that limit tracking while providing access, opportunity, and proactive intervention for students across all populations.

continued

Indicator	Stage 1 Leaders	Stage 2 Leaders	Stage 3 Leaders
3. Every teacher works interdependently in a collaborative learning community to erase inequities in student learning.	• Recognize, understand, and model the components of a professional learning community. • Develop a results-driven culture, and participate in a collaborative teacher team for mathematics program improvement.	• Collaborate with teachers to create the support and structures necessary to implement a professional learning community. • Support the learning of teachers to work as a professional learning community in order to monitor gains in student achievement for every student population.	• Advocate for and ensure a systemic implementation of a professional learning community throughout all aspects of the mathematics curriculum, instruction, and assessment at the school, district, regional, or provincial level.

Teaching and Learning Leadership

Principle 2: Ensure high expectations and access to meaningful mathematics instruction every day.

Indicator	Stage 1 Leaders	Stage 2 Leaders	Stage 3 Leaders
1. Every teacher pursues the successful learning of mathematics for every student.	• Develop and model knowledge about instructional strategies for improved student learning. • Identify student populations in need of additional support for success within the mathematics curriculum, and use strategies to meet the needs of those students.	• Engage teacher teams to collaboratively identify and implement common curricular outcomes. • Engage teacher teams in the collaborative development and implementation of instructional strategies needed to support every learner. • Ensure implementation of collaborative planning, common curriculum pacing, and improved instructional strategies by teacher teams.	• Ensure the implementation of a systemic plan for the continuous improvement of school, district, regional, or provincial student achievement across all populations. • Monitor and respond to the level of attainment of targeted student achievement benchmarks, and publicly celebrate results with the extended school community.
2. Every teacher implements research-informed best practices and uses effective instructional planning and teaching strategies.	• Develop and model knowledge of research-informed instructional strategies and best practices for effective student learning of mathematics. • Formulate and implement effective lesson planning to achieve intended learning goals. • Develop and model knowledge of tools necessary to assess the current status of teaching practices. • Recognize the importance of technology integration into the mathematics curriculum.	• Determine the current status of teacher knowledge and implementation of research-informed, effective instructional strategies. • Facilitate growth of teachers' mathematical knowledge and implementation of research-informed best practices. • Engage teachers in collaborative dialogue about research-informed instructional practices and planning for effective student learning of mathematics. • Collaborate with and support teachers in integrating technology into the mathematics curriculum.	• Ensure implementation of best-practice instruction in every student's learning experience throughout the district, region, or province. • Facilitate a systemic, continuous process of mathematics instructional improvement that reflects current research-informed practices. • Ensure the ongoing use of technology as an embedded and systemic part of the mathematics curriculum and instruction at the district, regional, or provincial level.

continued

Teaching and Learning Leadership (continued)

Indicator	Stage 1 Leaders	Stage 2 Leaders	Stage 3 Leaders
3. Every teacher participates in continuous and meaningful mathematics professional development and learning in order to improve his or her practice.	• Develop and use knowledge regarding research-informed best practices in mathematics professional learning. • Use current status of teachers' mathematical teaching and learning knowledge to identify areas for teacher improvement and growth. • Engage in professional learning and reflection as a model of self-assessment and growth.	• Engage every teacher in appropriate professional learning and reflection regarding mathematics content, pedagogy, and assessment. • Facilitate participation in collaborative site-based professional development and learning for every teacher.	• Implement a comprehensive professional development and learning plan for improved teacher growth and development throughout the district, region, or province. • Ensure necessary resources, time within the school day, and support for continuous professional development and learning are provided to every teacher throughout the district, region, or province.

Curriculum Leadership

Principle 3: Ensure relevant and meaningful mathematics in every lesson.

Indicator	Stage 1 Leaders	Stage 2 Leaders	Stage 3 Leaders
1. Every teacher implements the local curriculum and uses instructional resources are coherent and reflect state standards and national curriculum recommendations.	• Develop and apply knowledge of state standards and national curriculum recommendations and their impact on the local curriculum. • Recognize, understand, and model the connection between the coherence and focus of the local curriculum to effective instruction and achievement.	• Engage teachers and collaboratively develop local curriculum consistent with state standards. • Ensure coherent and consistent implementation of the local curriculum by all teachers.	• Ensure coherent implementation and ongoing review by district, regional, or provincial stakeholders for the alignment of local curriculum with state and national curriculum recommendations and assessments.
2. Every teacher implements a curriculum that is focused on relevant and meaningful mathematics.	• Develop awareness of, understand, and model the rationale, characteristics, and qualities of meaningful, relevant, and important mathematics. • Develop an awareness of and model the applications and connections within mathematics and other content areas.	• Engage teachers and teacher teams in developing and implementing meaningful and relevant mathematics curriculum for each course or grade level.	• Ensure the collective analysis and continuous systemic improvement of the implemented local curriculum throughout the district, region, or province.

continued

64

Becoming a PRIME Leader

Curriculum Leadership (continued)

Indicator	Stage 1 Leaders	Stage 2 Leaders	Stage 3 Leaders
3. Every teacher implements the intended curriculum with needed intervention and makes certain it is attained by every student.	• Examine and model the congruence among the intended curriculum, the implemented curriculum, and the attained curriculum.	• Engage teachers and teacher teams in identifying and acting on inconsistencies among the intended, implemented, and attained curriculum. • Engage teachers and teacher teams in developing and implementing vertically aligned curriculum.	• Ensure congruence between the developed and implemented curriculum throughout the district, regional, or provincial mathematics programs. • Participate in the systemic development, implementation, and student attainment of a well-articulated, rigorous, and coherent preK–12 mathematics curriculum throughout the district, region, or province.

Assessment Leadership

Principle 4: Ensure timely, accurate monitoring of student learning and adjustment of teacher instruction for improved student learning.

Indicator	Stage 1 Leaders	Stage 2 Leaders	Stage 3 Leaders
1. Every teacher uses student assessments that are congruent and aligned by grade level or course content.	• Ensure assessment measures important mathematics—mathematics that is relevant and serves as critical underpinning for future learning. • Recognize and model the importance of aligning content expectations and instructional practices with the form and content of assessment. • Recognize and model a response to inequities created by inconsistent assessment instruments and inappropriate grading practices.	• Ensure teachers provide students the opportunity to learn the mathematics to be assessed. • Collaboratively ensure alignment between school and district assessments with state standards and national curriculum recommendations. • Participate in and lead teams in school- and district-level development of common assessments and scoring rubrics to ensure alignment with instructional practice.	• Engage in the periodic review and updating of local, regional, or provincial assessments to respond to changing conditions and insights gained from prior assessment. • Provide teachers, teacher teams, and administrators with requisite professional development and learning about assessment literacy. • Facilitate and conduct effective public dialogue about the role, process, development, and results of assessments with all stakeholders at the district, regional, or provincial level.
2. Every teacher uses formative assessment processes to inform teacher practice and student learning.	• Use multiple sources of student assessment data to help teachers inform and improve their teaching practice. • Learn and model the use of formative assessment and its impact on student learning.	• Assist teachers and teacher teams in developing and implementing formative assessments that will optimize opportunities for every student to learn.	• Create and support structures that allow teams of teachers at the district, regional, or provincial level to collectively analyze assessment data to enhance student learning. • Develop and monitor a systemic district, regional, or provincial process through which teachers provide students with timely, ongoing, and meaningful feedback.

continued

Indicator	Stage 1 Leaders	Stage 2 Leaders	Stage 3 Leaders
2. Every teacher uses formative assessment processes to inform teacher practice and student learning.	• Recognize and model the importance of ongoing student feedback as a part of the student learning process.	• Facilitate effective teacher dialogue and interdependent practice regarding the implementation of formative assessment and ongoing student feedback.	• Inform administrators, parents, and the education community of assessment results from multiple sources of data.
3. Every teacher uses summative assessment data to evaluate mathematics grade level, course, and program effectiveness.	• Develop and model an understanding of summative assessment and its impact on student learning. • Ensure all assessments are constructed to maximize the likelihood students can demonstrate the mathematics they know. • Recognize and model the importance of ongoing student feedback as a part of the student learning process.	• Engage teachers and teacher teams in meaningful dialogue about large-scale local, state, and national assessment data and how to use the data to inform practice. • Assist teachers and teacher teams in developing and implementing summative assessments that will optimize opportunities for every student to learn. • Engage teachers in collaborative discussions regarding the use of summative assessment data to improve student learning.	• Facilitate use of local, state, and national summative assessment data in evaluating the continuous improvement and effectiveness of the local mathematics program. • Implement and monitor a systemic process to ensure that all summative assessments are fair and free of bias at the district, regional, or provincial level. • Inform administrators, parents, and the extended education community of assessment results from multiple sources of data.

Next Steps: Using the Framework

In the most successful schools, teachers supported by administrators take initiative to improve school-wide policies and programs, teaching and learning, and communication. By understanding the phenomenon of teacher leadership and helping teachers develop the skills required to act as leaders, we will improve schools and help teachers realize their full potential.

—Danielsen, 2007, p. 19

Leadership is complex, and without a leadership framework, efforts toward student improvement can be unfocused and chaotic. The PRIME framework answers the questions, "What does an effective mathematics education leader need to know?" and "What does an accomplished leader do?" in order to provide a context and structure for leadership discussions that will result in improved teacher and student learning. The framework may be applied in the following ways:

A structure for focused improvement efforts. The PRIME Leadership Framework provides a template for creating and evaluating mathematics program initiatives to target improvement efforts within the scope of human capital and resources available.

A path for novice leaders. New leaders will need to be prepared in the knowledge and skills necessary to promote leadership principles in equity, teaching and learning, curriculum, and assessment. The leadership framework provides a focus for teacher educators as they structure graduate school programs for future teacher leadership.

Guidance for the recruitment and hiring of new mathematics leaders in schools. The selection of department chairs, school and district curriculum leaders, grade-level or course team leaders, coaches and mentors, and other mathematics leadership positions can be informed by the coherent definition of leadership provided in this framework. Districts can use the PRIME Leadership Framework to develop and shape their own concept of effective teacher leadership standards throughout the school.

A tool for communication with the extended education community. A focused effort for leadership driven by PRIME standards can be shared with the extended educational community to secure information and support for district or provincial mathematics expectations for student learning and teacher leadership.

Reflective guidance for experienced leaders. The framework can provide a professional "audit" of leadership practice and effort for all levels of mathematics leadership positions and roles. See the Self-Evaluation Rubrics and Reflective Questions (pages 69–80) for further guidance.

Self-Evaluation and Questions for the Reflective Practitioner and Leader

The questions and self-evaluation rubrics in this section are based on each of the 12 leadership indicators outlined in the PRIME Framework. They are designed to inspire thoughtful reflection and discussion by individuals or groups of preservice teacher leaders (graduate students), practicing teachers, teacher coaches and mentors, department chairs, principals, district leaders, teacher educators, grade- or course-level team leaders, professional development and learning leaders, and others with an interest in and commitment to improving the leadership in equity, teaching and learning, curriculum, and assessment.

Use these questions, individually or with a leadership team, to consider leadership issues from your professional work experiences and assess your progress on the Stage 1 or Stage 2 continuum for each indicator. A blank framework for each principle has been provided for you to record your current status. Use the frameworks to create a plan of staff development and learning growth actions to close the gap between where you are now and your leadership ideal for that indicator, then decide if you are ready for some Stage 3 leadership actions for a specific leadership principle.

Self-Evaluation Rubric for PRIME Equity Leadership

Principle 1: Ensure high expectations and access to meaningful mathematics learning for every student.

What is my progress on the PRIME indicators for Equity Leadership? To what extent does my leadership ensure:	STAGE 1 Know and Model				STAGE 2 Collaborate and Implement			
	I have no understanding and have taken no action. 1	I have a basic understanding. 2	I have deep understanding. 3	I use my understanding to take action and model for others. 4	I develop awareness in others, but often inconsistently. 1	I ensure collaborative discussion by teams. 2	I follow discussion with collaborative action by teacher teams. 3	I systematically and intentionally ensure complete implementation by all teachers and teaching teams. 4
1. Every teacher addresses gaps in mathematics achievement expectations for all student populations?								
2. Every teacher provides each student access to relevant and meaningful mathematics experiences?								
3. Every teacher works independently in a collaborative learning community to erase inequities in student learning?								

Reflective Questions for PRIME Equity Leadership

Stage 1 and 2 Current Status
Based on pages 9–20, and the actions summary on pages 60–61, what specific actions or behaviors support your self-evaluation of PRIME Equity Leadership for each indicator?

Indicator 1: _____

_____

_____

Indicator 2: _____

_____

_____

Indicator 3: _____

_____

_____

Stage 1 and 2 Leadership Growth Strategy
What specific strategies could you use to advance your PRIME Equity Leadership for each indicator?

Indicator 1: _____

_____

_____

Indicator 2: _____

_____

_____

Indicator 3: _____

_____

_____

continued

Reflective Questions for PRIME Equity Leadership
(continued)

Stage 3 Readiness, Commitment, and Participation

Leaders at Stage 3 choose to advocate for and deepen systemic implementation of the PRIME Equity Leadership indicators. Although it should be the aim of every mathematics education leader to pursue and experience the full impact of Stage 2 leadership, actions and experiences in Stage 3 could lead to broader and deeper discussions and expanded awareness that subsequently generate new knowledge for Stages 1 and 2. In what specific ways can you advocate for and grow your sphere of influence regarding each of the PRIME Equity Leadership indicators?

Indicator 1: _____

_____

_____

Indicator 2: _____

_____

_____

Indicator 3: _____

_____

_____

© 2008 National Council of Supervisors of Mathematics • *The PRIME Leadership Framework*
http://ncsmonline.org • www.solution-tree.com

Self-Evaluation Rubric for PRIME Teaching and Learning Leadership

Principle 2: Ensure high expectations and access to meaningful mathematics instruction every day.

What is my progress on the PRIME indicators for Teaching and Learning Leadership? To what extent does my leadership ensure:	STAGE 1 Know and Model				STAGE 2 Collaborate and Implement			
	I have no understanding and have taken no action.	I have a basic understanding.	I have deep understanding.	I use my understanding to take action and model for others.	I develop awareness in others, but often inconsistently.	I ensure collaborative discussion by teams.	I follow discussion with collaborative action by teacher teams.	I systematically and intentionally ensure complete implementation by all teachers and teaching teams.
	1	2	3	4	1	2	3	4
1. Every teacher pursues the successful learning of mathematics for every student?								
2. Every teacher implements research-informed best practices and uses effective instructional planning and teaching strategies?								
3. Every teacher participates in continuous and meaningful mathematics professional development and learning in order to improve his or her practice?								

Reflective Questions for PRIME Teaching and Learning Leadership

Stage 1 and 2 Current Status

Based on pages 21–31 and the actions summary on pages 62–63, what specific actions or behaviors support your self-evaluation of PRIME Teaching and Learning Leadership for each indicator?

Indicator 1: _____

_____

_____

Indicator 2: _____

_____

_____

Indicator 3: _____

_____

_____

Stage 1 and 2 Leadership Growth Strategy

What specific strategies could you use to advance your PRIME Teaching and Learning Leadership for each indicator?

Indicator 1: _____

_____

_____

Indicator 2: _____

_____

_____

Indicator 3: _____

_____

_____

continued

Reflective Questions for PRIME Teaching and Learning Leadership (continued)

Stage 3 Readiness, Commitment, and Participation

Leaders at Stage 3 choose to advocate for and deepen systemic implementation of the PRIME Teaching and Learning Leadership indicators. Although it should be the aim of every mathematics education leader to pursue and experience the full impact of Stage 2 leadership, actions and experiences in Stage 3 could lead to broader and deeper discussions and expanded awareness that subsequently generate new knowledge for Stages 1 and 2. In what specific ways can you advocate for and grow your sphere of influence regarding each of the PRIME Teaching and Learning Leadership indicators?

Indicator 1: _____

_____

_____

Indicator 2: _____

_____

_____

Indicator 3: _____

_____

_____

Self-Evaluation Rubric for PRIME Curriculum Leadership

Principle 3: Ensure relevant and meaningful mathematics in every lesson.

What is my progress on the PRIME indicators for Curriculum Leadership? To what extent does my leadership ensure:	STAGE 1 Know and Model				STAGE 2 Collaborate and Implement			
	I have no understanding and have taken no action. 1	I have a basic understanding. 2	I have deep understanding. 3	I use my understanding to take action and model for others. 4	I develop awareness in others, but often inconsistently. 1	I ensure collaborative discussion by teams. 2	I follow discussion with collaborative action by teacher teams. 3	I systematically and intentionally ensure complete implementation by all teachers and teaching teams. 4
1. Every teacher implements the local curriculum and uses instructional resources that are coherent and reflect state standards and national curriculum recommendations?								
2. Every teacher implements a curriculum that is focused on relevant and meaningful mathematics?								
3. Every teacher implements the intended curriculum with needed intervention and makes certain it is attained by every student?								

Reflective Questions for PRIME Curriculum Leadership

Stage 1 and 2 Current Status

Based on pages 33–43 and the actions summary on pages 64–65, what specific actions or behaviors support your self-evaluation of PRIME Curriculum Leadership for each indicator?

Indicator 1: _____

_____

_____

Indicator 2: _____

_____

_____

Indicator 3: _____

_____

_____

Stage 1 and 2 Leadership Growth Strategy

What specific strategies could you use to advance your PRIME Curriculum Leadership for each indicator?

Indicator 1: _____

_____

_____

Indicator 2: _____

_____

_____

Indicator 3: _____

_____

_____

continued

Reflective Questions for PRIME Curriculum Leadership
(continued)

Stage 3 Readiness, Commitment, and Participation

Leaders at Stage 3 choose to advocate for and deepen systemic implementation of the PRIME Curriculum Leadership indicators. Although it should be the aim of every mathematics education leader to pursue and experience the full impact of Stage 2 leadership, actions and experiences in Stage 3 could lead to broader and deeper discussions and expanded awareness that subsequently generate new knowledge for Stages 1 and 2. In what specific ways can you advocate for and grow your sphere of influence regarding each of the PRIME Curriculum Leadership indicators?

Indicator 1: _____

_____

_____

Indicator 2: _____

_____

_____

Indicator 3: _____

_____

_____

Self-Evaluation Rubric for PRIME Assessment Leadership

Principle 4: Ensure timely, accurate monitoring of student learning and adjustment of teacher instruction for improved student learning.

What is my progress on the PRIME indicators for Assessment Leadership? To what extent does my leadership ensure:	STAGE 1 Know and Model				STAGE 2 Collaborate and Implement			
	I have no understanding and have taken no action. 1	I have a basic understanding. 2	I have deep understanding. 3	I use my understanding to take action and model for others. 4	I develop awareness in others, but often inconsistently. 1	I ensure collaborative discussion by teams. 2	I follow discussion with collaborative action by teacher teams. 3	I systematically and intentionally ensure complete implementation by all teachers and teaching teams. 4
1. Every teacher uses student assessments that are congruent and aligned by grade level or course content?								
2. Every teacher uses formative assessment processes to inform teacher practice and student learning?								
3. Every teacher uses summative assessment data to evaluate mathematics grade-level, course, and program effectiveness?								

Reflective Questions for PRIME Assessment Leadership

Stage 1 and 2 Current Status

Based on pages 45–54 and the actions summary on pages 66–67, what specific actions or behaviors support your self-evaluation of PRIME Assessment Leadership for each indicator?

Indicator 1: _____

_____

_____

Indicator 2: _____

_____

_____

Indicator 3: _____

_____

_____

Stage 1 and 2 Leadership Growth Strategy

What specific strategies could you use to advance your PRIME Assessment Leadership for each indicator?

Indicator 1: _____

_____

_____

Indicator 2: _____

_____

_____

Indicator 3: _____

_____

_____

continued

Reflective Questions for PRIME Assessment Leadership

(continued)

Stage 3 Readiness, Commitment, and Participation

Leaders at Stage 3 choose to advocate for and deepen systemic implementation of the PRIME Assessment Leadership indicators. Although it should be the aim of every mathematics education leader to pursue and experience the full impact of Stage 2 leadership, actions and experiences in Stage 3 could lead to broader and deeper discussions and expanded awareness that subsequently generate new knowledge for Stages 1 and 2. In what specific ways can you advocate for and grow your sphere of influence regarding each of the PRIME Assessment Leadership indicators?

Indicator 1: _____

_____

_____

Indicator 2: _____

_____

_____

Indicator 3: _____

_____

_____

References

■ ■ ■ ■

Carpenter, T. P., & Lehrer, R. (1999). Teaching and learning mathematics with understanding. In E. Fennema & T. A. Romberg (Eds.), *Mathematics classrooms that promote understanding* (pp. 19–32). Mahwah, NJ: Lawrence E. Erlbaum Associates.

Chrispeels, J., Strait, J., & Brown, J. (1999). The paradoxes of collaboration: What works. *Educational Leadership, 29*(2), 16–19.

Chu Clewell, B. (1999). In National Council of Supervisors of Mathematics, *Mathematics for all: A sourcebook of essential information for leaders in mathematics equity* (pp. iv–32). Golden, CO: Author.

Conzemius, A., & O'Neill, J. (2001). *Building shared responsibility for student learning.* Alexandria, VA: Association for Supervision and Curriculum Development.

Danielson, C. (2007). The many faces of leadership. *Education Leadership, 65*(1), 14–19.

Darling-Hammond, L. (1996). What matters most: A competent teacher for every child. *Phi Delta Kappan, 78*(3), 193–200.

Darling-Hammond, L. (2006). If they'd only do their work! *Educational Leadership, 63*(5), 8–13.

DuFour, R., Eaker, R., & DuFour, R. (Eds.). (2005). *On common ground: The power of professional learning communities.* Bloomington, IN: Solution Tree (formerly National Educational Service).

Elmore, R. (2004). *School reform from the inside out: Policy, practice and performance.* Cambridge, MA: Harvard University Press.

Elmore, R. (2007). Let's act like professionals. *Journal of Staff Development, 28*(3), 31–32.

Fennema, E. (1999). Mathematics teachers in transition. In National Council of Supervisors of Mathematics, *Mathematics for all: A sourcebook of essential information for leaders in mathematics equity* (pp. iv–45). Golden, CO: Author.

Ferrini-Mundy, J., Graham, K., Johnson, L., & Mills, G. (1998). *Making change in mathematics education: Learning from the field.* Reston, VA: National Council of Teachers of Mathematics.

Flores, A. (2007, October/November). Examining disparities in mathematics education: Achievement gap or opportunity gap? *High School Journal, 91*(1), 29–42.

Fullan, M. (2007). Change the terms of teacher learning. *Journal of Staff Development, 28*(3), 35–36.

Glickman, C. (2002). *Leadership for learning: How to help teachers succeed.* Alexandria, VA: Association for Supervision and Curriculum Development.

Goleman, D., Boyatzis, R., & McKee, A. (2002). *Primal leadership: Realizing the power of emotional intelligence.* Boston: Harvard Business School Press.

Haycock, K. (2001). Closing the achievement gap. *Educational Leadership, 58*(6), 6–11.

Haberman, M. (1997, March). Unemployment training: The ideology of nonwork learned in urban schools. *Phi Delta Kappan, 78*(7), 499–503.

Kouzes, J., & Posner, B. (2006). *A leader's legacy.* San Francisco: Jossey-Bass.

Lambert, L. (1998). *Building leadership capacity in schools.* Alexandria, VA: Association for Supervision and Curriculum Development.

Little, J. W. (1990). The persistence of privacy: Autonomy and initiative in teachers' professional relations. *Teachers College Record, 91*(4), 509–536.

Loucks-Horsley, S., Hewson, P. W., Love, N., & Stiles, K. E. (1998). *Designing professional development for teachers of science and mathematics.* Thousand Oaks, CA: Corwin Press.

Marzano, R. (2007). *The art and science of teaching: A comprehensive framework for effective instruction.* Alexandria, VA: Association for Supervision and Curriculum Development.

Marzano, R., Waters, T., & McNulty, B. (2005). *School leadership that works: From research to results.* Alexandria, VA: Association for Supervision and Curriculum Development.

National Commission on Mathematics and Science Teaching for the 21st Century. (2000). *Before it's too late: A report to the nation from the national commission on mathematics and science teaching for the 21st century.* Washington, DC: Author.

National Commission on Teaching and America's Future. (2003). *No dream denied: A pledge to America's children.* Washington, DC: Author.

National Council of Supervisors of Mathematics. (1999). *Mathematics for all: A sourcebook of essential information for leaders in mathematics equity.* Golden, CO: Author.

National Council of Teachers of Mathematics. (2000). *Principles and standards for school mathematics.* Reston, VA: Author.

National Council of Teachers of Mathematics. (2006). *Curriculum focal points for prekindergarten through grade 8 mathematics: A quest for coherence.* Reston, VA: Author.

National Council of Teachers of Mathematics. (2007). *Mathematics teaching today.* Reston, VA: Author.

National Research Council. (2001). *Adding it up: Helping children learn mathematics.* Washington, DC: National Academy Press.

National Staff Development Council. (2001). *Standards for staff development.* Oxford, OH: Author.

Oakes, J. (1985). *Keeping track: How schools structure inequality.* New Haven, CT: Yale University Press.

Reeves, D. (2004). *Assessing educational leaders: Evaluating performance for improved individual and organizational results.* Thousand Oaks, CA: Corwin Press.

Reeves, D. (2005). Putting it all together: Standards, assessments, and accountability in successful professional learning communities. In R. DuFour, R. Eaker, & R. DuFour (Eds.), *On common ground: The power of professional learning communities* (pp. 45–63). Bloomington, IN: Solution Tree (formerly National Educational Service).

Reeves, D. (2006). *The learning leader: How to focus school improvement for better results.* Alexandria, VA: Association for Supervision and Curriculum Development.

Romberg, T., & Kaput, J. (1999). Mathematics worth teaching, mathematics worth understanding. In E. Fennema & T. Romberg (Eds.), *Mathematics classrooms that promote understanding* (pp. 3–17). Mahwah, NJ: Lawrence E. Erlbaum Associates.

Saphier, J. (2005). Masters of motivation. In R. DuFour, R. Eaker, & R. DuFour (Eds.), *On common ground: The power of professional learning communities* (pp. 85–113). Bloomington, IN: Solution Tree (formerly National Educational Service).

Sparks, D. (2005). Leading for transformation in teaching, learning, and relationships. In R. DuFour, R. Eaker, & R. DuFour (Eds.), *On common ground: The power of professional learning communities* (pp. 155–175). Bloomington, IN: Solution Tree (formerly National Educational Service).

Spillane, J., Halverson, R., & Diamond, J. (2004). Towards a theory of leadership practice: A distributed perspective. *Journal of Curriculum Studies, 36*(1), 3–34.

Stiggins, R. (2002). Assessment crisis: The absence of assessment FOR learning. *Phi Delta Kappan, 83*(10), 758–765.

Stiggins, R., Arter, J., Chappuis, J., & Chappuis, S. (2006). *Classroom assessment for student learning: Doing it right—Using it well.* Princeton, NJ: Educational Testing Service.

Strutchens, M. E. (2000). Confronting beliefs and stereotypes that impede the mathematical empowerment of African American students. In M. E. Strutchens, M. Johnson, & W. Tate (Eds.), *Changing the faces of mathematics: Perspectives on African Americans* (pp. 7–14). Reston, VA: National Council of Teachers of Mathematics.

Strutchens, M. E., Lubienski, S., McGraw, R., & Westbrook, S. K. (2004). NAEP findings regarding race/ethnicity: Students' performance, school experiences, attitudes and beliefs, and family influences. In P. Kloosterman & F. K. Lester (Eds.), *Results and interpretations of the 1990 through 2000 mathematics assessments of the National Assessment of Educational Progress* (pp. 269–304). Reston, VA: National Council of Teachers of Mathematics.

Teddlie, C., & Stringfield, S. (1993). *Schools do make a difference: Lessons learned from a 10-year study on school effects.* New York: Teachers College Press.

Wilkins, A., & Education Trust Staff. (2006). *Yes, we can: Telling truths and dispelling myths about race and education in America.* Washington, DC: Education Trust. Retrieved November 20, 2006 from www2.edtrust. org/NR/rdonlyres/DD58DD01-23A4-4B89-9FD8-C11BB072331E/0/ YesWeCan.pdf

Additional Resources for Leadership Development and Support

■ ■ ■ ■

Equity

Anderson, C. R. (2007). Examining school mathematics through the lenses of learning and equity. In W. G. Martin, M. E. Strutchens, & P. C. Elliott (Eds.), *The learning of mathematics* (pp. 97–112). Reston, VA: National Council of Teachers of Mathematics.

Bishop, A. J., & Forgasz, H. J. (2007). Issues in access and equity in mathematics education. In F. K. Lester, Jr. (Ed.), *Second handbook of research on mathematics teaching and learning.* (pp. 1145–1168). Charlotte, NC: Information Age Publishing.

Darling-Hammond, L. (1997). *The right to learn: A blueprint for creating schools.* San Francisco: Jossey-Bass.

DuFour, R., & Eaker, R. (1998). *Professional learning communities at work: Best practices for enhancing student achievement.* Bloomington, IN: Solution Tree (formerly National Educational Service).

DuFour, R., Eaker, R., & DuFour, R. (Eds.). (2005). *On common ground: The power of professional learning communities.* Bloomington, IN: Solution Tree (formerly National Educational Service).

DuFour, R., DuFour, R., Eaker, R., & Many, T. (2006). *Learning by doing: A handbook for professional learning communities at work.* Bloomington, IN: Solution Tree.

Edwards, C. (Ed.). (1999). *Changing the faces of mathematics: Perspectives on Asian Americans and Pacific Islanders.* Reston, VA: National Council of Teachers of Mathematics.

Fennema, E., Carpenter, T., & Sowder, J. (1999). Creating classrooms that promote understanding. In E. Fennema & T. Romberg (Eds.), *Mathematics classrooms that promote understanding* (pp. 185–199). Mahwah, NJ: Lawrence E. Erlbaum Associates.

Ferrini-Mundy, J., Graham, K., Johnson, L., & Mills, G. (1998). *Making change in mathematics education: Learning from the field.* Reston, VA: National Council of Teachers of Mathematics.

Hankes, J., & Fast, G. (Eds.). (2002). *Changing the faces of mathematics: Perspectives on indigenous people of North America.* Reston, VA: National Council of Teachers of Mathematics.

Jacobs, J., Rossi-Becker, J., & Gilmer, G. (Eds.). (2001). *Changing the faces of mathematics: Perspectives on gender.* Reston, VA: National Council of Teachers of Mathematics.

National Research Council. (2004). *How students learn mathematics in the classroom.* Washington, DC: National Academy Press.

The nation's report card: NAEP 2005. (2005). Washington, DC: U.S. Department of Education, National Center for Education Statistics.

Oakes, J. (1990). *Multiplying inequalities: The effects of race, social class, and tracking on opportunities to learn mathematics and science.* Santa Monica, CA: RAND Corporation.

Ortiz-Franco, L., Hernandez, N., & de la Cruz, Y. (Eds.). (1999). *Changing the faces of mathematics: Perspectives on Latinos.* Reston, VA: National Council of Teachers of Mathematics.

Secada, W. G. (1992). Race, ethnicity, social class, language, and achievement in mathematics. In D. A. Grouws (Ed.), *Handbook of research on mathematics teaching and learning* (pp. 623–660). New York: Macmillan.

Secada, W. (Ed.). (1999). *Changing the faces of mathematics: Perspectives on multiculturalism and gender equity.* Reston, VA: National Council of Teachers of Mathematics.

Secada, W., Fennema, E., & Byrd, L. (Eds.). (1995). *New directions for equity in mathematics education.* New York: Cambridge University Press.

Sergiovanni, T. J. (2005). *Strengthening the heartbeat: Leading and learning together in schools.* San Francisco: Jossey-Bass.

Strutchens, M., Johnson, M., & Tate, W. (Eds.). (2000). *Changing the faces of mathematics: Perspectives on African Americans.* Reston, VA: National Council of Teachers of Mathematics.

Teaching and Learning

National Council of Supervisors of Mathematics. (2007). *Improving student achievement by leading sustained professional learning for mathematics content and pedagogical knowledge.* Denver, CO: Author.

Rubenstein, R. N. (2004). *Perspectives on the teaching of mathematics.* Reston, VA: National Council of Teachers of Mathematics.

Curriculum

Elmore, R. F. (2000). *Building a new structure of school leadership.* New York: Albert Shanker Institute.

English, F. (2000). *Deciding what to teach and test: Developing, aligning, and auditing the curriculum.* Thousand Oaks, CA: SAGE.

Franklin, C., et al. (2005). *Guidelines for assessment and instruction in statistics education (GAISE) report: A pre-K–12 curriculum framework.* Alexandria, VA: American Statistical Association.

Fullan, M. (2001). *Leading in a culture of change.* San Francisco: Jossey-Bass.

Garver, J. (2005). *The ten secrets to higher student achievement.* Phoenix, AZ: All Star Publications.

Hirsch, C. (Ed.). (2007). *Perspectives on the design and development of school mathematics curricula.* Reston, VA: National Council of Teachers of Mathematics.

Lester, F. (2007). *Second handbook of research on mathematics teaching and learning.* Charlotte, NC: National Council of Teachers of Mathematics, Information Age Publishing.

Loucks-Horsley, S., Love, N., Stiles, K. E., Munday, S., Newson, P. W. (2003). *Designing professional development for teachers of science and mathematics* (2nd ed.). Thousand Oaks, CA: Corwin Press.

Marzano, R. (2005). *School leadership that works: From research to results.* Aurora, CO: Mid-continent Research for Education and Learning.

Nasir, N. S., & Cobb, P. (Eds.). (2007). *Improving access to mathematics: Diversity and equity in the classroom.* New York: Teachers College Press

National Assessment Governing Board. (2004). *Mathematics framework for the 2005 national assessment of educational progress.* Washington, DC: U.S. Department of Education.

Reys, B. J. (Ed.). (2006). *The intended mathematics curriculum as represented in state-level curriculum standards: Consensus or confusion?* Charlotte, NC: Information Age Publishing.

Senk, S., & Thompson, D. (2003). *Standards-based school mathematics curricula: What are they? What do students learn?* Mahwah, NJ: Lawrence E. Erlbaum Associates.

Assessment

American Institutes for Research. (2007). *A field guide to student success in mathematics and science.* Washington, DC: Author.

Corallo, C., & McDonald, D. (2002). *What works with low-performing schools: A review of research.* Charleston, WV: Appalachia Educational Laboratory.

Huinker, D., & Collins, A. (Eds.). (2006). *Prekindergarten–grade 2 mathematics assessment sampler.* Reston, VA: National Council of Teachers of Mathematics.

Kloosterman, P., & Lester, F. (Eds.). (2007). *Results and interpretations of the 2003 mathematics assessment of the National Assessment of Educational Progress.* Reston, VA: National Council of Teachers of Mathematics.

Langer, G., Colton, A., & Goff, L. (2003). *Collaborative analysis of student work.* Alexandria, VA: Association for Supervision and Curriculum Development.

Mathematical Sciences Education Board, National Research Council. (1993a). *Measuring UP: Prototypes for mathematics assessment.* Washington, DC: National Academy Press.

Mathematical Sciences Education Board, National Research Council. (1993b). *Measuring what counts: A conceptual guide for mathematics assessment.* Washington, DC: National Academies Press.

National Council of Teachers of Mathematics. (1995). *Assessment standards for school mathematics.* Reston, VA: Author.

National Council of Teachers of Mathematics. (2007). *Research clips: What is formative assessment?* Reston, VA: Author.

Pellegrino, J., Chudousky, N., & Glaser, R. (Eds.). (2001). *Knowing what students know: The science and design of educational assessment.* Washington, DC: National Research Council.